YORK NOTES

D1335485

AN INSPECTOR CALLS

J. B. PRIESTLEY

WORKBOOK BY MARY GREEN

PEARSON

YORK PRESS

The right of Mary Green to be identified as the Author of this Work has been asserted by her in accordance with the Copyright, Designs and Patents Act 1988

YORK PRESS
322 Old Brompton Road, London SW5 9JH

PEARSON EDUCATION LIMITED
Edinburgh Gate, Harlow,
Essex CM20 2JE, United Kingdom
Associated companies, branches and representatives throughout the world

First published 2014

10 9 8 7 6 5 4 3 2 1

ISBN 978–1–4479–8045–2

Illustrations by Philip Harris; and Neil Gower (page 6 only)

Photo credits:
Jalcaraz/Shutterstock.com for page 8 / Joachim Wendler/Shutterstock.com for page 10 / Susan Law Cain/Shutterstock.com for page 23 / Super3D/Shutterstock.com for page 27 / Seqoya/Shutterstock.com for page 49 / sergign/Shutterstock.com for page 51

Typeset by Carnegie Book Production
Printed in Slovakia

CONTENTS

PART FOUR:
KEY CONTEXTS AND THEMES

PART FIVE:
LANGUAGE AND STRUCTURE

PART SIX:
GRADE BOOSTER

PART ONE: INTRODUCTION

How to use this workbook

WHAT IS THE WORKBOOK FOR?

This workbook is for your use during your study or revision of *An Inspector Calls.* It can be used on its own, or alongside the York Notes for GCSE: *An Inspector Calls* study guide, which is available in bookshops or online at www.yorknotes.com. It will help you:

- **Revise** the basic content of the play – who did what? When? Where? Why?

- **Practise** key reading and writing skills, such as writing more fluent paragraphs

- **Assess** your own level by seeing other students' work and comments from experts on it

WHY A WORKBOOK?

By providing 'Progress logs', and space to write in your answers for many of the tasks, the workbook gives you a visual indication of how well you are doing. You could even share it with your English teacher if you want!

HOW IS THE WORKBOOK ORGANISED?

The workbook is divided into six main Parts and follows the same basic structure as the York Notes study guide if you want to cross-refer between them. You can:

- Follow the parts one by one, checking your knowledge and skills in stages

Or

- Dip in, selecting areas you feel most, or least, confident about

WHAT ARE THE KEY FEATURES?

There are **'Quick tests'** designed to check your knowledge through short, quick tasks such as multiple choice or 'true/false' questions.

'Thinking more deeply' requires you to write more fully (often a sentence or two) about a particular issue or character.

'Exam preparation' goes a bit further and requires you to deal with full-length questions, and plan and draft part of an exam-style answer with support to help you.

A **'Progress log'** at regular intervals allows you to keep a running record of how you are doing.

At the end of each section there is a **'Practice task'**, which gives you an even more challenging task to complete in full, as revision for your exam.

'Answers' for most tasks are supplied at the end of the workbook, but try not to look at them while you're completing the tasks, however much you are tempted! Wait until you have had one or even two attempts before you check.

Most importantly, enjoy using this workbook and see your knowledge and skills improve!

The text used in this workbook is the Heinemann edition, 1992.

Introducing *An Inspector Calls*

Before you begin this workbook, check how well you know *An Inspector Calls*.

SETTING

1 Look at the illustrations below. On each illustration write the names of characters and events linked to each location. For example, you could write 'where Eva Smith was taken after her suicide' on Hospital/Mortuary.

The Birlings' House — where the Birlings live + the dinner party is held

The Police Station — where the inspector came from

where the inspector comes to interrogate everyone

The Factory — where Eva Smith used to work before being fired by mr Birling

where Eva used to work before sheila got her fired — *MILWARDS*

Palace Variety Theatre — where Eva met Gerald and Eric

Hospital/Mortuary — where Eva was taken after her suicide

CHARACTERS: WHO'S WHO

❷ Now look at these drawings of the different characters. Without checking the play or the York Notes study guide, complete the name of each person:

Mrs _Birling_

Inspector _Goole_

Eva _smith_

Gerald Croft

Mr _Birling_

sheila Birling

Eric Birling

J. B. PRIESTLEY: AUTHOR AND CONTEXT

❸ What do you know about J. B. Priestley and the context in which *An Inspector Calls* was written? Circle the correct information in each sentence:

a) In <u>1908 / 1905 / 1906</u> the Labour Party is established.

b) Priestley joins the 10th Duke of Wellington's Regiment in WWI and fights in <u>Belgium / France / Britain</u>.

c) Priestley goes to <u>Cambridge / Oxford / Durham</u> in 1919 to study political science and literature.

d) Priestley is a journalist in London. His essays called *Brief <u>Diversions / Departures / Directions</u>* are published in 1922.

e) The General Strike involves nationwide industrial action in <u>1924 / 1926 / 1928</u>.

f) In <u>1929 / 1927 / 1931</u> America's stock market in Wall Street crashes and there is an economic depression.

g) Priestley writes *English <u>Journey / Rambles / Sojourn</u>* after travelling through the poverty-stricken parts of England.

h) Priestley works for BBC Radio during the Second World War (1939–45). He publishes *Britain Speaks,* a series of <u>talks / essays / stories</u>.

i) In <u>1945 / 1943 / 1947</u> *An Inspector Calls* is written; Labour wins the General Election and atomic bombs are dropped on Hiroshima and Nagasaki in Japan.

PART TWO: PLOT AND ACTION

Act One, Part 1: The dinner party (pp. 1–7)

QUICK TEST

❶ Which of these are **TRUE** statements about this scene, and which are **FALSE**? Write 'T' or 'F' into the boxes:

a) The stage directions indicate that the Birling family are warm hearted and loving. `F`

b) We are told that Mr Birling is of a higher social class than his wife. `F`

c) Mr Birling is pleased that Gerald is to become part of the family. `T`

d) Sheila reminds Gerald that he neglected her last summer. `T`

e) Eric is slightly drunk at the dinner party. `T`

f) Mrs Birling is disappointed with Sheila's engagement ring. `F`

g) Mr Birling is concerned that there will soon be trouble with the workforce. `F`

THINKING MORE DEEPLY

❷ Write **one** or **two sentences** in response to each of these questions:

a) What do you learn about the social position of the Birling family?

when we are first introduced to the birling family we (as the audience are ~~told~~ shown that they are an upper class family.   Why?

b) What impression do we get of Sheila and Gerald's relationship?

Sheila and Gerald are a very happyly engaged couple but as the play continues we see that they drift further apart - until sheila is unsure whether she wants to marry him.

c) What do we learn about Eric from his behaviour at the dinner party?

At the dinner party Eric is acting quite 'squiffy' as said by sheila - implying that he is drunk and eventuall

EXAM PREPARATION: WRITING ABOUT WHAT MR BIRLING REPRESENTS

Re-read Mr Birling's monologues (speeches) (pp. 6–7) from *'There's a good deal of silly talk'* to *'which will always be behindhand naturally.'*

Question: How do Mr Birling's comments help you to understand attitudes amongst many of the wealthy before the First World War?

Think about:

- How he regards himself and those in his position
- What he thinks the future will hold

❸ Complete this table:

Point/detail	Evidence	Effect or explanation
1: *He believes the powerful and wealthy should protect their position.*	*'We employers at last are coming together to see that our interests … are properly protected.'*	*His comments imply that he disregards the workforce he employs.*
2: *He likes to speak at length and expects to be listened to.*		
3: *He is confident that future technology will bring prosperity.*		

❹ Write up **point 1** into a **paragraph** below, in your own words:

....

....

....

....

....

....

❺ Now, choose **one** of your **other points** and write it out as another **paragraph** here:

....

....

....

....

....

....

....

PROGRESS LOG [tick the correct box]   Needs more work ☐   Getting there ☐   Under control ☐

Act One, Part 2: Mr Birling confides in Gerald (pp. 7–11)

QUICK TEST ✔

❶ Choose the correct answer to **finish the statement** and tick the box:

a) Mr Birling held the position of: Chief Constable ☐   Lord Mayor ☑   Member of Parliament ☐

b) Mr Birling expects to receive a: knighthood ☑   royal visit ☐   visit from Lady Croft ☐

c) Gerald and Mr Birling joke about a: possible death ☐   possible scandal ☑   visit from the Inspector ☐

d) Mrs Birling and Sheila are discussing: Lady Croft ☐   clothes ☑   Eric ☐

e) Eric arouses curiosity when he: refuses to join the men for port ☐   claims not to remember something ☑   leaves by the back door ☐

THINKING MORE DEEPLY ?

❷ Write **one** or **two sentences** in response to each of these questions:

a) How do we know that Mr Birling feels inferior to Gerald's family?

....

....

....

b) How does Gerald behave with Mr Birling in this scene?

....

....

....

c) How can we tell there is something wrong with Eric before the Inspector arrives?

....

....

....

EXAM PREPARATION: WRITING ABOUT MR BIRLING'S ATTITUDES

Re-read Mr Birling's speech (p. 8) from *'I was Lord Mayor here'* to *'chance of a knighthood'* and his speech (pp. 9–10) from *'don't want to lecture'* to *'and look after himself and his own'*.

Question: What do Mr Birling's comments reveal about his character?

Think about:

- What he says about himself and what he expects

- What he says about the community

❸ Complete this table:

Point/detail	Evidence	Effect or explanation
1: *He believes he will be knighted (for contributions to the community).*	*'I've always been regarded as a sound useful party man.'*	*His comments suggest that a knighthood will depend on his support for the right people and political party.*
2: *He believes in self reliance.*		
3: *He has no respect for the community.*		

❹ Write up **point 1** into a **paragraph** below, in your own words:

....

....

....

....

....

....

❺ Now, choose **one** of your **other points** and write it out as another **paragraph** here:

....

....

....

....

....

....

....

PROGRESS LOG [tick the correct box]   Needs more work ☐   Getting there ☐   Under control ☐

Act One, Part 3: The enquiry begins (pp. 11–16)

QUICK TEST

❶ Complete this **gap-fill** paragraph about the scene, adding the **correct or suitable information**:

We first meet Inspector .... when Edna, the maid, announces him.

Although not a .... man, he is an imposing figure. Mr Birling tries to

impress the Inspector by pointing out that he was an alderman and also Lord

Mayor and still sits on the ...., meaning he is a magistrate. The

Inspector explains that a girl died in the Infirmary after swallowing strong

.... A letter and a diary were found in her room. She had more than

one name, but her original name was .... and she worked at Mr

Birling's .... The Inspector shows Mr Birling a .... of the

girl. Eventually Mr Birling remembers that he sacked her because of her part in a

.... for higher wages.

THINKING MORE DEEPLY ❓

❷ Write **one** or **two sentences** in response to each of these questions:

a) Why do you think Mr Birling wanted to impress the Inspector?

....

....

....

....

b) What does Gerald think about Eva Smith's sacking?

....

....

....

....

c) What does the Inspector mean by 'a chain of events' (p. 14)?

....

....

....

....

....

EXAM PREPARATION: WRITING ABOUT DIFFERENT POINTS OF VIEW

Re-read the dialogue (p. 15) from *'**Inspector:** It's my duty to ask questions'* to *'**Inspector:** … to ask for the earth than to take it.'*

Question: What different points of view do Mr Birling and Eric hold about Eva Smith's sacking?

Think about:

- What each character says
- What each character cares about

❸ Complete this table:

Point/detail	Evidence	Effect or explanation
1: *Mr Birling cares about the profit his company makes.*	*'it's my duty to keep labour costs down'.*	*His comments tell us that he values the profit he makes more than a good wage for his workers.*
2: *Eric is sympathetic to the hardship Eva Smith faced.*		
3: *We can further compare Mr Birling and Eric's points of view about taking responsibility for the workers.*		

❹ Write up **point 1** into a **paragraph** below, in your own words:

....

....

....

....

....

....

❺ Now, choose **one** of your **other** points and write it out as another **paragraph** here:

....

....

....

....

....

....

....

PROGRESS LOG [tick the correct box]   Needs more work ☐   Getting there ☐   Under control ☐

Act One, Part 4: Sheila's sympathy turns to shock (pp. 16–21)

QUICK TEST ✓

❶ Who is each character talking **about**? Write a **name** (or names) from the list below next to each quotation:

Sheila   Eva Smith   the Inspector   Eric   Gerald   factory workers

a) '**Birling:** … I've half a mind to report you. I've told you all I know –' **(p. 17)**

....

b) '**Sheila:** *(rather distressed)* Sorry! It's just that I can't help thinking about this girl –' **(p. 17)**

....

c) '**Gerald:** … It's what happened to her since she left Mr Birling's works that is important.' **(p. 18)**

....

d) '**Birling:** And are you suggesting now that one of them knows something about this girl?' **(p. 18)**

....

e) '**Sheila:** But these girls aren't cheap labour – they're *people*.' **(p. 19)**

....

f) '**Eric:** She recognized her from the photograph, didn't she?' **(p. 21)**

....

g) '**Birling:** *(angrily)* Why the devil do you want to go upsetting the child like that?' **(p. 21)**

....

THINKING MORE DEEPLY ?

❷ Write **one** or **two sentences** in response to each of these questions:

a) In what way does the Inspector drive home the awfulness of Eva Smith's death?

....
....
....

b) How does Mr Birling's mood change when he realises all the family might be involved with Eva Smith?

....
....
....

c) Why does the Inspector show the photograph to one character at a time?

....
....
....

EXAM PREPARATION: WRITING ABOUT SHEILA'S INVOLVEMENT

Re-read (pp. 19–21) from '**Inspector:** *Where was I before Mr Croft*' to the stage directions '*The other three stare in amazement for a moment.*'

Question: In what way is Sheila involved with Eva Smith and how does she react to the knowledge?

Think about:

● What Sheila says and feels

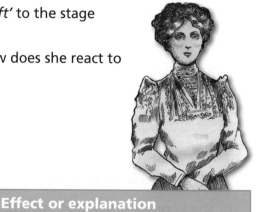

❸ Complete this table:

Point/detail	Evidence	Effect or explanation
1: *Sheila scolds her father for sacking Eva Smith.*	*'I think it was a mean thing to do. Perhaps that spoilt everything for her.'*	*She not only feels sympathy for Eva Smith but also recognises the possible consequences of her father's actions.*
2: *Sheila begins to realise that Eva is the girl she had sacked from Milwards.*		
3: *Sheila recognises the girl in the photograph the Inspector shows her.*		

❹ Write up **point 1** into a **paragraph** below, in your own words:

....

....

....

....

....

....

❺ Now, choose **one** of your **other points** and write it out as another **paragraph** here:

....

....

....

....

....

....

....

PROGRESS LOG [tick the correct box]   Needs more work ☐   Getting there ☐   Under control ☐

Act One, Part 5: Sheila and the shop girl (pp. 21–6)

QUICK TEST ✓

❶ Which of these are **TRUE** statements about this scene, and which are **FALSE**? Write 'T' or 'F' into the boxes:

a) Mr Birling exits to tell his wife what is happening. ☐

b) Gerald doesn't want to look at the photograph and refuses to do so. ☐

c) The Inspector suggests Eric had better stay in the room. ☐

d) Sheila refuses to accept she is partly to blame for Eva Smith's downfall. ☐

e) Sheila insists that Eva Smith made unpleasant comments in Milwards. ☐

f) The Inspector is trying to understand why Eva Smith died. ☐

g) Sheila immediately recognises that Gerald knew Daisy Renton. ☐

THINKING MORE DEEPLY ?

❷ Write **one** or **two sentences** in response to each of these questions:

a) Why did Sheila have Eva Smith dismissed?

....

....

....

....

....

....

b) How can we tell in this scene that Sheila regrets what happened at Milwards?

....

....

....

....

....

....

c) What is dramatic about the ending to Act One?

....

....

....

....

....

EXAM PREPARATION: WRITING ABOUT THE INSPECTOR'S POWER

Re-read (pp. 21–2) from the stage directions *'BIRLING looks as if about to make some retort'* to *'Inspector: … Just as your father is.'*

Question: How is the Inspector gaining control and power over the situation?

Think about:

- What the character says and the tone he uses
- How he manages the other characters

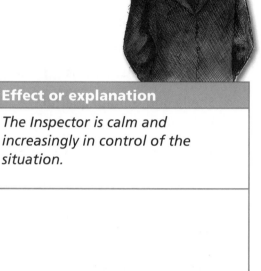

❸ Complete this table:

Point/detail	Evidence	Effect or explanation
1: *The Inspector deliberately refuses Gerald's request.*	*'Gerald: I'd like to have a look at that photograph now, Inspector.'* *'Inspector: All in good time.'*	*The Inspector is calm and increasingly in control of the situation.*
2: *He states his opinion regardless of whom he is speaking to.*		
3: *He states the consequences of Eva Smith's dismissal from Milwards.*		

❹ Write up **point 1** into a **paragraph** below, in your own words:

....

....

....

....

....

....

❺ Now, choose **one** of your **other points** and write it out as **another paragraph** here:

....

....

....

....

....

....

....

PROGRESS LOG [tick the correct box]   Needs more work ☐   Getting there ☐   Under control ☐

Act Two, Part 1: Sharing the guilt (pp. 27–9)

QUICK TEST ✓

❶ Choose the correct answer to finish the statement and tick the box:

a) Act Two opens: in the garden ☐   in the hall ☐   where Act One finished ☐

b) At the beginning of Act Two the Inspector is: in the doorway ☐
sitting down ☐   leaving the stage ☐

c) Initially, Sheila: frowns ☐   laughs hysterically ☐   wipes her tears ☐

d) Sheila and Gerald: quarrel ☐   do not speak to each other ☐
leave the room together ☐

e) The Inspector: interrupts Gerald and Sheila ☐   arrests Gerald ☐   goes out ☐

f) Mrs Birling enters: with the maid ☐   unaware of the situation ☐   with Eric ☐

g) At first, Mrs Birling approaches the Inspector: politely ☐   rudely ☐   fearfully ☐

h) Mrs Birling: does not understand Sheila ☐   thinks Sheila is ill ☐
sees Sheila crying ☐

THINKING MORE DEEPLY ?

❷ Write one or two sentences in response to each of these questions:

a) What is Gerald afraid of?

b) What does Mrs Birling attempt to do when she enters?

c) How does Sheila react to her mother and what is she afraid of?

EXAM PREPARATION: WRITING ABOUT SHEILA'S CHANGING ATTITUDES

Re-read (pp. 27–9) from **'Inspector:** Well, I don't want to keep you here' to **'Sheila:** ...
I don't understand about you.'

Question: In this scene, how does Sheila come to regard her own part in Eva Smith's death?

Think about:

- What she says and how she feels

- What she needs to discover about herself and the other characters

③ Complete this table:

Point/detail	Evidence	Effect or explanation
1: *Sheila suspects that Gerald is also implicated in Eva Smith/Daisy Renton's death.*	*She says to the Inspector: 'you haven't finished asking questions – have you? ...Then I'm staying.'*	*She wants to hear the truth, even if it is unpleasant.*
2: *But she still feels she is to blame.*		
3: *The Inspector discusses shared responsibility.*		.

④ Write up **point 1** into a **paragraph** below, in your own words:

....

....

....

....

....

....

⑤ Now, choose **one** of your **other points** and write it out as **another paragraph** here:

....

....

....

....

....

....

....

PROGRESS LOG [tick the correct box]   Needs more work ☐   Getting there ☐   Under control ☐

Act Two, Part 2: Mrs Birling bustles in (pp. 29–32)

QUICK TEST

1 Complete this **gap-fill** paragraph about the scene, with the **correct or suitable information**:

Mrs Birling enters in a .... manner, which is very different to the mood of the others in the room. When Mrs Birling comments that the Inspector has made an impression on her ...., he replies that this often happens with the young. Sheila is determined to stay, despite her mother's comment that Sheila has a morbid curiosity about the girl's .... As the scene develops, Mrs Birling's self-importance increases and she accuses the Inspector of being .... She reminds him that .... was once Lord Mayor. However, she is shocked to learn of the seriousness of .... drinking habit.

THINKING MORE DEEPLY

2 Write **one** or **two sentences** in response to each of these questions:

a) In what way does the word 'offence' have a double meaning?

....
....
....
....
....

b) Why does the Inspector question Mrs Birling about Eric's drinking?

....
....
....
....
....

c) How does Gerald respond to Mrs Birling's question about Eric's drinking?

....
....
....
....

EXAM PREPARATION: WRITING ABOUT SHEILA'S FOREWARNING

Re-read the dialogue (pp. 30–1) from *'Sheila: (urgently cutting in) Mother, don't –* *please don't.'* to *'Mrs Birling: ... Inspector will take offence – '.*

Question: Why does Sheila use the image of a 'wall' to address her mother and how does her mother respond?

Think about:

- How Sheila uses the image
- How her mother responds

❸ Complete this table:

Point/detail	Evidence	Effect or explanation
1: Sheila is aware that Mrs Birling does not accept that the family may have played a part in Eva Smith's death.	'You mustn't try to build up a kind of wall between us and that girl.'	The 'wall' describes the way in which Mrs Birling separates herself (and her family and Gerald) from possible guilt.
2: Sheila is warning her mother what will happen if she fails to answer the Inspector's questions.		
3: Mrs Birling fails to understand.		

❹ Write up **point 1** into a **paragraph** below, in your own words:

....
....
....
....
....
....

❺ Now, choose **one** of your **other points** and write it out as another **paragraph** here:

....
....
....
....
....
....

PROGRESS LOG [tick the correct box]   Needs more work ☐   Getting there ☐   Under control ☐

Act Two, Part 3: Gerald's confession (pp. 32–40)

QUICK TEST ✔

❶ From the list of names, identify which **character** is being **referred to**. Sometimes it might be more than one person.

Sheila   Gerald   Daisy Renton/Eva Smith   Eric   Alderman Meggarty

a) '**Birling:** I've been trying to persuade …….. to go to bed, but he won't.' **(p. 32)**

b) '**Birling:** What's the matter with <u>that child</u>?' **(p. 33)**

c) '**Inspector:** … Mr Croft, when did you first get to know <u>her</u>?' **(p. 33)**

d) '**Sheila:** Well, we didn't think <u>you</u> meant Buckingham Palace.' **(p. 34)**

e) '**Gerald:** <u>He's</u> a notorious womanizer [and] one of the worst sots and rogues in Brumley –' **(p. 35)**

f) '**Inspector:** Yes. <u>She</u> was a woman. She was lonely. Were <u>you</u> in love with her?' **(p. 37)**

g) '**Sheila**: …<u>You</u> were the wonderful Fairy Prince.' **(p. 38)**

THINKING MORE DEEPLY

❷ Write **one** or **two sentences** in response to each of these questions:

a) How does Gerald's confession affect the audience?

b) How does Sheila help create the idea that the Inspector is all-knowing?

c) How does Sheila react to Gerald at the end of the scene?

EXAM PREPARATION: WRITING ABOUT THE INSPECTOR'S KNOWLEDGE

Re-read the dialogue (p. 39) from *'**Gerald:** Yes, we'd agreed about that.'* to
*'**Inspector:** Go where? Home?'*

Question: How does the Inspector appear to know so much about people and
events? How is Gerald affected by the Inspector's knowledge?

Think about:

- The Inspector's methods, e.g. use of the diary

- How Gerald responds

❸ Complete this table:

Point/detail	Evidence	Effect or explanation
1: *The Inspector asks simple questions.*	*He asks questions of Gerald such as: 'When did this affair end?'; 'How did she take it?'; 'She had to move out of those rooms?'*	*These questions, which often build on what the characters say, encourage the characters to reveal further events and actions.*
2: *Gerald is curious about the Inspector's knowledge.*		
3: *Gerald reacts to the information about Daisy Renton.*		

❹ Write up **point 1** into a **paragraph** below, in your own words:

....

....

....

....

....

....

❺ Now, choose **one** of your **other points** and write it out as another **paragraph** here:

....

....

....

....

....

....

....

PROGRESS LOG [tick the correct box]   Needs more work ☐   Getting there ☐   Under control ☐

Act Two, Part 4: Sheila warns her mother (pp. 40–2)

QUICK TEST ✔

❶ Which of these are **TRUE** statements about this scene, and which are **FALSE**? Write 'T' or 'F' into the boxes:

a) Mr Birling tries to defend Eric to Sheila. ☐

b) Sheila points out that the Inspector did not show Gerald the photograph. ☐

c) Mrs Birling does not wish to look at the photograph. ☐

d) Sheila defends her mother against the Inspector. ☐

e) Eric returns with Gerald to speak to Mr Birling. ☐

f) Mrs Birling chairs the Charity for Homeless Animals. ☐

g) Mr and Mrs Birling are concerned that Eric has gone out. ☐

THINKING MORE DEEPLY ?

❷ Write **one** or **two sentences** in response to each of these questions:

a) How does Gerald react to parting from Sheila?

b) How is the photograph used in this scene?

c) In what way does the Inspector's authority increase in this scene?

EXAM PREPARATION: Writing about social position

Re-read the dialogue (pp. 41–2) from *'Inspector: You're not telling me the truth.'* to *'Sheila: … And can't you see, both of you, you're making it worse?'*

Question: How does J. B. Priestley challenge the Birlings's idea of their own superiority in this scene?

Think about:

- What Mr Birling says
- What the Inspector says
- What Sheila says

❸ Complete this table:

Point/detail	Evidence	Effect or explanation
1: *The Inspector demands the truth from Mrs Birling.*	*Mr Birling demands an apology but the Inspector counters: 'Apologize for what – doing my duty?'*	*The Inspector is not threatened by Mr Birling.*
2: *The Inspector reminds Mr Birling of his duties.*		
3: *Sheila challenges her parents' haughtiness.*		

❹ Write up **point 1** into a **paragraph** below, in your own words:

....

....

....

....

....

....

❺ Now, choose **one** of your **other points** and write it out as **another paragraph** here:

....

....

....

....

....

....

....

PROGRESS LOG [tick the correct box]   Needs more work ☐   Getting there ☐   Under control ☐

Act Two, Part 5: The deserving and the undeserving (pp. 42–9)

QUICK TEST ✓

❶ Choose the correct answer to **finish the statement** and tick the box:

a) Mr Birling returns: with Eric ☐   to say that Eric has left ☐
to say that Gerald has left ☐

b) Mrs Birling claims Eric was: over-excited ☐   sober and sensible ☐   asleep ☐

c) Mrs Birling saw Eva Smith: a year ago ☐   last September ☐   two weeks ago ☐

d) The Committee: refused to help Eva Smith ☐   argued about Eva Smith ☐
gave Eva Smith money ☐

e) Mrs Birling: did not attend the committee ☐   was chair of the committee ☐
was an ordinary member of the committee ☐

f) Sheila says that her mother is: an honest woman ☐   dignified ☐   cruel ☐

g) Eva Smith refused to take: stolen money ☐   assistance from the Birlings ☐
food ☐

THINKING MORE DEEPLY ❓

❷ Write **one** or **two sentences** in response to each of these questions:

a) What is Mrs Birling's attitude to Eva Smith at the committee meeting?

....
....
....
....

b) What is Mr Birling's attitude to his wife's treatment of Eva Smith?

....
....
....
....

c) Who does Mrs Birling insist is the main culprit in Eva Smith's death and what effect does this have?

....
....
....
....

EXAM PREPARATION: WRITING ABOUT THE CHAIN OF EVENTS

Re-read the dialogue (pp. 43–9) from *'Inspector: She appealed to your organization for help?'* to the end of the Act.

Question: What clues does J. B. Priestley give us about where the chain of events will take us?

Think about:

- The women's charity hearing and Mrs Birling's attitude
- What Sheila and the Inspector say

③ Complete this table:

Point/detail	Evidence	Effect or explanation
1: *Eva Smith's name changes for a third time.*	*Mrs Birling says, 'First, she called herself Mrs Birling –'.*	*This implies that Eric (the only character left to be questioned) was involved with Eva.*
2: *Eva Smith was pregnant.*		
3: *Sheila warns her mother not to insist that the father of Eva Smith's child should take responsibility.*		

④ Write up **point 1** into a **paragraph** below, in your own words:

....
....
....
....
....
....

⑤ Now, choose **one** of your **other points** and write it out as another **paragraph** here:

....
....
....
....
....
....

PROGRESS LOG [tick the correct box]   Needs more work ☐   Getting there ☐   Under control ☐

Act Three, Part 1: Eric in the spotlight (pp. 50–2)

QUICK TEST ✔

❶ Write the correct names by each quotation to show **who is speaking and to whom**:

Mr Birling	Sheila	Eric	Mrs Birling	the Inspector	Gerald

a) 'There must be some mistake.' **(p. 50)**

.... to ....

b) 'You haven't made it any easier for me' **(p. 50)**

.... to ....

c) 'you're not the type – you don't get drunk –' **(p. 50)**

.... to ....

d) 'Why, you little sneak!' **(p. 50)**

.... to ....

e) 'I could have told her months ago' **(p. 50)**

.... to ....

f) 'Where did you meet her?' **(p. 51)**

.... to ....

g) 'And I couldn't remember her name' **(p. 52)**

.... to ....

THINKING MORE DEEPLY ?

❷ Write **one** or **two sentences** in response to each of these questions:

a) At the start of the scene Eric says, 'You know, don't you?' What does he mean?

....

....

....

....

b) Mr Birling accuses Sheila of being disloyal. What does this tell you about him?

....

....

....

....

c) When does Mrs Birling's mood change in this scene and what happens?

....

....

....

....

EXAM PREPARATION: WRITING ABOUT ERIC

Re-read the dialogue (pp. 51–2) from '**Inspector:** (To Eric) 'When did you first meet this girl?' to '**Eric:** … Oh – my God! – how stupid it all is!'

Question: In this scene, what does Eric's account of his first meeting with Eva Smith tell you about him?

Think about:

- Where he was and what he says about himself

- How he reacts to the Inspector's questions

❸ Complete this table:

Point/detail	Evidence	Effect or explanation
1: *Eric had been drinking.*	*'I'd been there [in the Palace Bar] an hour or so with two or three chaps. I was a bit squiffy.'*	*His judgement would be impaired and his behaviour unstable.*
2: *He became increasingly drunk.*		
3: *He had sex with Eva Smith.*		

❹ Write up **point 1** into a **paragraph** below, in your own words:

....

....

....

....

....

....

❺ Now, choose **one** of your **other points** and write it out as another **paragraph** here:

....

....

....

....

....

....

PROGRESS LOG [tick the correct box]   Needs more work ☐   Getting there ☐   Under control ☐

Act Three, Part 2: A baby on the way (pp. 52–3)

QUICK TEST

❶ Complete this **gap-fill** paragraph about the scene, with the **correct or suitable information**:

Eric explains that he met Eva Smith again about .... weeks later by accident at the .... He says that they talked, and explains that he was not in love with her. .... is angry because Eric slept with Eva Smith again. The two men quarrel, but the .... intervenes in order to continue questioning .... Eric admits that when he discovered that Eva Smith was pregnant, he was worried about what would happen to him. He says that Eva Smith did not wish to .... him, and that he gave her money, about .... pounds in total.

THINKING MORE DEEPLY

❷ Write **one** or **two sentences** in response to each of these questions:

a) What was Eric's attitude to Eva Smith *after his first meeting with her*?

....

....

....

....

....

b) How can we tell that Eric's attitude to Eva Smith shifted as he got to know her?

....

....

....

....

....

c) How can we tell that Eric is immature?

....

....

....

....

EXAM PREPARATION: WRITING ABOUT LANGUAGE

Re-read the dialogue (p. 52) from '**Inspector:** *But you took her home again?*' to '**Eric:** *– the ones I see some of your respectable friends with –*'.

Question: In this scene, how does the language alter when the female characters have left, and what conclusions do you draw from this?

Think about:

- What each male character present says
- How this compares with any earlier comments

③ Complete this table:

Point/detail	Evidence	Effect or explanation
1: *Mr Birling uses language more freely in male company.*	*'So you had to go to bed with her?'*	*In 1912 a man like Mr Birling would not refer to sexual matters at all in front of women of his class.*
2: *The Inspector alters his language in male company.*		
3: *We can compare Eric's earlier language with the language he uses in male company.*		

④ Write up **point 1** into a **paragraph** below, in your own words:

....

....

....

....

....

....

⑤ Now, choose **one** of your **other points** and write it out as another **paragraph** here:

....

....

....

....

....

....

....

PROGRESS LOG [tick the correct box]   Needs more work ☐   Getting there ☐   Under control ☐

Act Three, Part 3: 'Fire and blood and anguish' (pp. 53–6)

QUICK TEST ✓

❶ Which of these are **TRUE** statements about this scene, and which are **FALSE**? Write 'T' or 'F' into the boxes:

a) Mr Birling is pleased that Eric acknowledges his duty to Eva Smith. ☐

b) Mrs Birling is shocked that Eric stole money. ☐

c) Sheila tells Eric that their mother met Eva Smith. ☐

d) Eric accuses his mother of not trying to understand him. ☐

e) Mr Birling accuses Eric of being hysterical. ☐

f) The Birlings are overcome with grief and fall silent. ☐

g) The Inspector explains that no crime has been committed. ☐

THINKING MORE DEEPLY ❓

❷ Write **one** or **two sentences** in response to each of these questions:

a) What is Mr Birling's main concern regarding what Eric has done?

....

....

....

....

....

b) How does the Inspector stress the chain of events that caused Eva Smith's suicide?

....

....

....

....

....

c) How has the mood changed since the beginning of Act One and why?

....

....

....

....

....

EXAM PREPARATION: WRITING ABOUT THE MESSAGE

Re-read the dialogue (p. 56) from '***Inspector:*** *You're offering the money'* to
'***Inspector:*** *... Good night.'*

Question: What is the message of the Inspector's speech before he leaves?

Think about:

- What the Inspector says about Eva Smith
- How he uses the example of Eva Smith to make a wider point

❸ Complete this table:

Point/detail	Evidence	Effect or explanation
1: *The Inspector reminds the Birlings that Eva Smith is dead and gone.*	*'You can't do her any more harm. And you can't do her any good now, either. You can't even say "I'm sorry, Eva Smith."'*	*It's too late to make amends to Eva Smith for the wrongs done to her.*
2: *He points out that there are others like Eva Smith.*		
3: *He warns of trouble for the future.*		

❹ Write up **point 1** into a **paragraph** below, in your own words:

....

....

....

....

....

....

❺ Now, choose **one** of your **other points** and write it out as another **paragraph** here:

....

....

....

....

....

....

....

PROGRESS LOG [tick the correct box]   Needs more work ☐   Getting there ☐   Under control ☐

Act Three, Part 4: A lesson not learnt (pp. 57–61)

QUICK TEST ✔

❶ Choose the correct answer to **complete the statement** and tick the box:

a) When the Inspector exits Sheila is: crying ☐   laughing hysterically ☐
   pacing up and down ☐

b) When the Inspector exits Mr Birling: shouts ☐   collapses ☐
   pours himself a drink ☐

c) Mr Birling is afraid he will not: make money ☐   become Mayor ☐
   get a knighthood ☐

d) Mrs Birling is ashamed of: Gerald ☐   the Inspector ☐   Eric ☐

e) Mr Birling tells Eric he could: go to court ☐   be called to the Mayor ☐
   be sent away ☐

f) Eric agrees with the views of: his father ☐   his mother ☐   his sister ☐

g) The Inspector ☐   Gerald ☐   Eric ☐ returns at the end of the scene.

THINKING MORE DEEPLY ?

❷ Write **one** or **two sentences** in response to each of these questions:

a) Why does Mr Birling turn on Eric?

....

....

....

....

b) How are we first alerted to the possibility that Inspector Goole may not be an
   inspector at all?

....

....

....

....

c) Why does Sheila take no comfort from the possibility that the Inspector is not a
   real one?

....

....

....

....

EXAM PREPARATION: WRITING ABOUT DIVISIONS IN THE FAMILY

Re-read the dialogue (pp. 57–8) from *'Sheila: I behaved badly too.'* to *'Eric: ... I didn't notice you told him that it's every man for himself.'*

Question: In what way are the younger and older generation divided in their views?

Think about:

- What Mr Birling, Sheila and Eric say
- How Mr Birling and Sheila refer to what has happened in different ways
- What Eric reminds his father of

3 Complete this table:

Point/detail	Evidence	Effect or explanation
1: *Sheila is aware of the important consequences of what has happened.*	*'But now you're beginning all over again to pretend nothing much happened –'.*	*She points out to her father that he is still not facing his share of the blame for Eva Smith's death.*
2: *Mr Birling's opinion of what has happened is different from Sheila's.*		
3: *Eric sarcastically reminds his father of his view that we should look after ourselves.*		

4 Write up **point 1** into a **paragraph** below, in your own words:

....

....

....

....

....

5 Now, choose **one** of your **other points** and write it out as another **paragraph** here:

....

....

....

....

....

....

PROGRESS LOG [tick the correct box]   Needs more work ☐   Getting there ☐   Under control ☐

Act Three, Part 5: Three telephone calls (pp. 61–72)

QUICK TEST ✔

❶ Write the correct names by each quotation to show *who* **is speaking** and *about* **whom.** Sometimes it might be more than one person.

Mr Birling   the Inspector   Sheila   Eric   Mrs Birling   Gerald   Eva Smith

a) 'he behaved in a very peculiar
   and suspicious manner.' (p. 61)   .... about ....

b) 'That man wasn't a police
   officer.' (p. 62)   .... about ....

c) 'I suppose we're all nice
   people now.' (p. 63)   .... about ....

d) 'I was the only one of you who
   didn't give in to him.' (p. 63)   .... about ....

e) 'Just remember your own
   position, young man.' (p. 64)   .... about ....

f) 'How do we know any girl
   killed herself today?' (p. 69)   .... about ....

g) 'you've argued this very
   cleverly.' (p. 70)   .... about ....

THINKING MORE DEEPLY ?

❷ Write **one** or **two sentences** in response to each of these questions:

a) What are the reasons behind Gerald's return?

   ....

   ....

   ....

   ....

b) Where does Eric place the theft in the list of his bad behaviour?

   ....

   ....

   ....

   ....

c) What does Mrs Birling seem to be most concerned about?

   ....

   ....

   ....

   ....

EXAM PREPARATION: WRITING ABOUT MOOD

Re-read the dialogue (pp. 69–72) beginning: *'Gerald: 'Anyway we'll see.''* to the stage directions *'the curtain falls.'*

Question: Discuss the range of the moods expressed and why in this scene.

Think about:

- How Mr Birling appears
- How Sheila reacts
- What happens at the very end of the play

③ Complete this table:

Point/detail	Evidence	Effect or explanation
1: *Gerald establishes there was no recent suicide of any young girls.*	*'Mr Birling: (triumphantly) There you are! Proof positive: The whole story's just a lot of moonshine.'*	*The tension lessens. Mr Birling becomes buoyant and jovial at the news.*
2: *Sheila cannot forget that a girl (or girls) was badly treated, regardless of who she was.*		
3: *There is a final telephone call to say an inspector is on his way.*		

④ Write up **point 1** into a **paragraph** below, in your own words:

....

....

....

....

....

....

⑤ Now, choose **one** of your **other points** and write it out as another **paragraph** here:

....

....

....

....

....

....

....

PROGRESS LOG [tick the correct box]   Needs more work ☐   Getting there ☐   Under control ☐

Practice task

❶ First, **read** this **exam-style** task:

Read the scene (pp. 8–11) in Act One from: **'*Birling:* Thanks. (Confidentially.) By the way'** to **'*Eric:* (defiantly) Nothing.'**

Question: What clues in this scene tell you there may be trouble ahead for the Birling family?

❷ Begin by circling the **key words** in the **question** above.

❸ Now, complete this table, noting down **3–4 key points** with **evidence** and the **effect** created:

Point	Evidence/quotation	Meaning or effect

❹ **Draft your response**. Use the space below for your first paragraph(s) and then continue onto a sheet of paper.

Start: *There are several clues in this scene that tell us there may be trouble ahead for the Birling family. Firstly,* ....

....

....

....

....

....

....

....

....

....

....

....

PROGRESS LOG [tick the correct box]   Needs more work ☐   Getting there ☐   Under control ☐

PART THREE: Characters

The Inspector

1 Each of the character traits below could be applied to the Inspector. Working from memory add points in the play when you think these are shown, then find at least one quotation to back up each idea:

Quality	Moment/s in play	Quotation
a) Principled		
b) Clever		
c) Inquiring		
d) Mysterious		

2 Look at this quotation from the Inspector. Add further annotations to it, by finding suitable adjectives from the bank at the bottom of the page, and explaining how J. B. Priestley's words help to convey the Inspector's character.

compelling – shows the Inspector's magnetism

Inspector: *(taking charge, masterfully)* Stop!

They are suddenly quiet, staring at him.

… <u>This girl killed herself – and died a horrible death. But each of you helped to kill her. Remember that. Never forget it</u>. […] You turned her away when she most needed help. <u>You refused her even the pitiable little bit of organized charity you had in your power to grant her.</u> (Act Three, p. 55)

> *hard-hitting*   *polite*   *all-knowing*   *trickster*   *compelling*   *sensitive*
>
> *articulate*   *commanding*   *intimidating*   *calm*

PROGRESS LOG [tick the correct box]   Needs more work ☐   Getting there ☐   Under control ☐

Mr Birling

❶ Look at the bank of **adjectives** describing Mr Birling. Circle the ones you think best **describe** him:

successful	ambitious	caring
popular	awkward	talkative
business-like	self-important	cruel
selfish	dishonest	unjust	middle-aged
shy	hard-headed	gracious

❷ Now add a **page reference** from your copy of the play next to each circle, showing where evidence can be found to **support** the **adjective**.

❸ Complete this **gap-fill** paragraph about Mr Birling, adding the **correct or suitable information**:

Mr Birling regards himself as a man of .... who has achieved a public position, such as that of Lord .... He is well-to-do, having made his money from .... but has little time for those who .... for him. His most important concern is to achieve a knighthood and he will do everything he can to prevent a .... from spoiling his chances. Mr Birling feels no remorse for .... Eva Smith. He is not affected by the words of the Inspector and when he discovers that the Inspector may not be what he seems, he even .... about the events surrounding the possible .... of Eva Smith.

❹ Using your **own judgement**, put a mark along this line to show **J. B. Priestley's overall presentation** of Mr Birling:

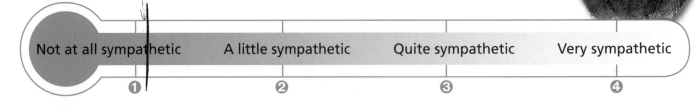

Not at all sympathetic	A little sympathetic	Quite sympathetic	Very sympathetic
➀	➁	➂	➃

PROGRESS LOG [tick the correct box]   Needs more work ☐   Getting there ☐   Under control ☐

Mrs Birling

1 Each of the character traits below could be applied to Mrs Birling. Working from memory add points in the play when you think these are shown, then find at least one quotation to back up each idea.

Quality	Moment/s in play	Quotation
a) Cold		
b) Prejudiced		
c) Unashamed		
d) Puritanical		

2 Look at this quotation from Mrs Birling. Add further annotations to it, by finding suitable adjectives from the bank at the bottom of the page, and explaining how J. B. Priestley's words help to convey Mrs Birling's character.

forceful – shows she is domineering

Mrs Birling: 'If you think you can bring <u>any pressure to bear upon me, Inspector,</u> <u>you're quite mistaken</u> … The girl asked for assistance … I wasn't satisfied with the girl's claim … and so <u>I used my influence to have it refused</u> … I consider I did my duty. So … <u>I prefer not to discuss it any further</u>' (Act Two, p. 44)

abrupt

prim-observed
ha :

unsympathetic to wards Eva, if she has a charity she shouldnt select who to help → she should help everyone

prim	*unsympathetic*	*abrupt*	*unloving*	*forceful*
ignorant	*self-righteous*	*powerful*	*arrogant*	

PROGRESS LOG [tick the correct box]   Needs more work ☐   Getting there ☐   Under control ☐

Sheila Birling

❶ Look at these statements about Sheila. For each one, decide whether it is **True [T]**, **False [F]** or whether there is **Not Enough Evidence [NEE]** to decide:

a) When we first meet Sheila she is described as a woman in her
mid-forties.   [T] [F] [NEE]

b) Sheila had never met the young woman before.   [T] [F] [NEE]

c) She had no idea the young woman's name was Eva Smith.   [T] [F] [NEE]

d) She is horrified by the revelation that a young woman has
committed suicide.   [T] [F] [NEE]

e) Sheila believes Eric will become a better man as a result of the
Inspector's visit.   [T] [F] [NEE]

f) Sheila hopes that her parents will come to understand the
Inspector's message.   [T] [F] [NEE]

g) Sheila is determined to marry Gerald come what may.   [T] [F] [NEE]

❷ Complete these statements about Sheila:

a) *Sheila is in a happy mood at the beginning of the play because ...* ....

....

....

....

b) *When she first meets the Inspector she realises that ...* ....

....

....

....

c) *Sheila is greatly affected by the Inspector's news, for example when ...* ....

....

....

....

d) *Of all the characters, Sheila changes the most and she is the one who ...* ....

....

....

....

e) *By the end of the play Sheila's relationship with Gerald ...* ....

....

....

....

PROGRESS LOG [tick the correct box]   Needs more work ☐   Getting there ☐   Under control ☐

Eric Birling

1 Without checking the book, write down from memory at least **two bits of information** we are told about Eric in each of these areas:

His background, age and manner	1: 2:
His behaviour and what he says or others say about him	1: 2:
His relationships	1: 2:

2 Now **check your facts**. Are you right? Look at the following pages:

His background, age and manner: (stage directions, pp. 1–2; Act One, p. 9)

His behaviour and what he says or others say about him: evidence of drinking (Act One, p. 3; Act Three, p. 51); response to Mr Birling (Act One, p. 16)

His relationships: with Mr Birling (Act One, pp. 9–11; Act Three, p. 54); with Mrs Birling (Act Three, pp. 50, 54–5); with Sheila (Act One, p. 5; Act Three, pp. 50, 64–5); with Eva Smith (Act Three, pp. 51–4)

3 What evidence can you find in Act Three that shows Eric has been affected by the Inspector's visit? In what way has he been affected? Think about:

- Eric's attitude to Eva Smith and her death

Find **evidence** in the text and include **quotations**.

Evidence	Quotation
a) *Eric is affected by what the Birlings did to Eva Smith.*	*'Eric: (shouting) And I say the girl's dead and we all helped to kill her – and that's what matters –'*
b) *Eric is affected by Eva Smith's …*	
c) *Eric despises …*	
d) *Eric agrees with Sheila …*	

PROGRESS LOG [tick the correct box]   Needs more work ☐   Getting there ☐   Under control ☐

Gerald Croft

1 Look at the bank of **adjectives** describing Gerald Croft. Circle the ones you think best **describe** him:

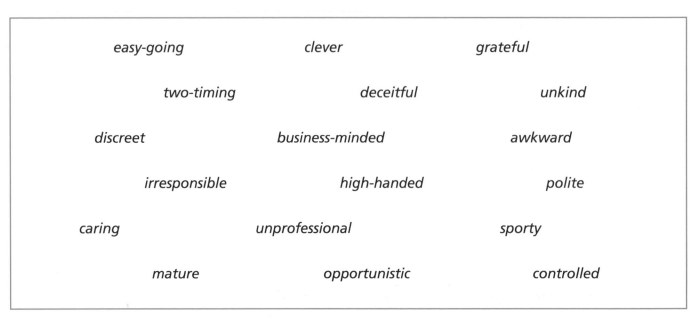

easy-going	clever	grateful
two-timing	deceitful	unkind
discreet	business-minded	awkward
irresponsible	high-handed	polite
caring	unprofessional	sporty
mature	opportunistic	controlled

2 Now add the **page reference** from your copy of the play next to each circle, showing where evidence can be found to **support** the **adjective**.

3 Complete this **gap-fill** paragraph about Gerald Croft, adding the **correct or suitable information**:

Gerald Croft belongs to the upper .... since his parents are Lord and Lady Croft. At the beginning of the play he is .... to Sheila Birling. .... considers Gerald to be a good catch not only because of his social position but also because he has a head for .... like himself. When Sheila discovers Gerald's affair with .... she is angry, but gives him credit for .... to the relationship. Gerald was genuinely fond of the young girl and is .... by her death. By the end of the play he hopes that .... will take him back.

4 Using your **own judgement**, put a mark along this line to show **J. B. Priestley's overall presentation** of Gerald Croft:

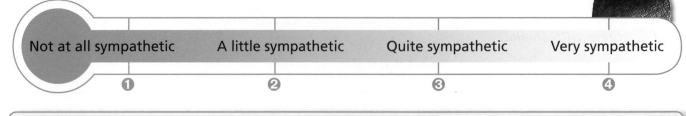

Not at all sympathetic	A little sympathetic	Quite sympathetic	Very sympathetic
❶	❷	❸	❹

PROGRESS LOG [tick the correct box]   Needs more work ☐   Getting there ☐   Under control ☐

Eva Smith/Daisy Renton

❶ Look at these statements about Eva Smith/Daisy Renton. For each one, decide whether it is **True [T]**, **False [F]** or whether there is **Not Enough Evidence [NEE]** to decide:

a) Eva Smith came from a country village. [T] [F] [NEE]

b) Eva Smith worked at Mr Birling's factory in the machine shop. [T] [F] [NEE]

c) She was a hard worker and likely to be promoted to a leading operator. [T] [F] [NEE]

d) She also worked at Milton's the hat shop. [T] [F] [NEE]

e) Despite her circumstances Eva Smith had principles. [T] [F] [NEE]

f) If she had the means, Eva Smith wanted to keep her baby. [T] [F] [NEE]

g) She wanted Eric to marry her when she discovered she was pregnant. [T] [F] [NEE]

❷ Complete these statements about Eva Smith:

a) *We never meet the girl who was called Eva Smith or Daisy Renton because …*

b) *However, we do know that a young girl (or girls) was badly treated by …*

c) *For example …*

d) *Gerald also knew the girl …*

e) *For J. B. Priestley, the girl represents …*

❸ Using your **own judgement**, put a mark along this line to show **J. B. Priestley's overall presentation** of Eva Smith/Daisy Renton:

Not at all sympathetic	A little sympathetic	Quite sympathetic	Very sympathetic
❶	❷	❸	❹

PROGRESS LOG [tick the correct box]   Needs more work ☐   Getting there ☐   Under control ☐

Practice task

1 First, **read** this **exam-style** task:

> Question: Do you think Gerald has changed or not by the end of the play?

2 Begin by circling the **key words** in the **question** above.

3 Now, complete this table, noting down **3–4 key points** with **evidence** and the **effect** created:

Point	Evidence/quotation	Meaning or effect

4 **Draft your response**. Use the space below for your first paragraph(s) and then continue onto a sheet of paper.

Start: *Gerald's role in the play...* ....

....

....

....

....

....

....

....

....

....

....

....

....

....

PROGRESS LOG [tick the correct box]   Needs more work ☐   Getting there ☐   Under control ☐

PART FOUR: KEY CONTEXTS AND THEMES

Key contexts

QUICK TEST ✔

❶ Choose the correct answer about the **context** of the play to **finish the statement** and tick the box:

a) The play is set in the fictional town of: Brough ☐   Brumley ☐   Burminster ☐

b) The stage directions tell us the Birling family are: in debt ☐   landowners ☐ prosperous ☐

c) Eva Smith lived: with her mother ☐   in lodgings ☐   on the streets ☐

d) The play: takes place in the Palace Variety Theatre ☐ takes place in the Birlings' home ☐   has more than one setting ☐

e) Milwards: is a thrift shop for the poor ☐   caters for the rich ☐   is a factory shop ☐

f) The play is set: before the First World War ☐   between the two World Wars ☐ in the 1950s ☐

THINKING MORE DEEPLY ❓

❷ Write **one** or **two sentences** in response to each of these questions:

a) How do we know from the start of the play (Act One, p. 2) that the Birlings see themselves as superior in status?

....

....

....

....

b) In Act Two we learn that Mr Birling's workers were discontented. Why were they unhappy and what happened as a result?

....

....

....

c) Why was a customer complaint enough to have Eva Smith sacked from Milwards, despite her being a good worker?

....

....

....

PROGRESS LOG [tick the correct box]   Needs more work ☐   Getting there ☐   Under control ☐

Key themes

QUICK TEST

❶ Complete this **gap-fill** paragraph about the scene, adding the **correct or suitable** information:

J. B. Priestley uses the Inspector as a way of showing how the ..young/women

in society are badly treated. He contrasts the easy, ..upper class *life of the*

Birlings with workers such as Eva Smith who struggle to survive, particularly

when ......work............ *is hard to get.*

The Inspector's message about our .... *to each other has little*

success with either .... *or* .... *However, his*

message affects ...Eric........... *who feels guilt and the need to change his*

behaviour. Sheila also accepts her guilt and the wider view that our lives are all

....

THINKING MORE DEEPLY

❷ Write **one** or **two sentences** in response to each of these questions about the **themes of love** and **time**:

a) What do you think Sheila learns about love by the end of the play?

By the end of the play it is clear that Sheila
feels differently about love and

b) In what ways are Eric's and Gerald's attitudes to Eva Smith the same?

Eric and Gerald are only know Eva because they
both had affairs with her, and their attitude
towards her is to protect her.

c) The play was first seen after the Second World War, but is set just before the First World War. Knowing this, how do you think the first audience felt? (Also consider the ending of the play.)

EXAM PREPARATION: WRITING ABOUT LOVE AND MARRIAGE

Re-read the beginning of the play (pp. 1–4) from the stage directions *'ARTHUR BIRLING is a heavy-looking, rather portentous man'* to **'Birling:** *... for lower costs and higher prices.'*

Question: What do you think Mr Birling's attitude to marriage is and what effect might this have had on his own marriage?

Think about:

- Mr Birling's attitude to Sheila and Gerald's marriage

- What Mrs Birling says

❸ Complete this table:

Point/detail	Evidence	Effect or explanation
1: *Mr Birling is pleased that his family and the Crofts will unite in marriage.*	'we may look forward to the time when Crofts and Birlings ... are working together — for lower costs and higher prices.'	*His hopes for Sheila's marriage are largely to do with the marriage of the two businesses*
2: *Mrs Birling comes from a higher class than her husband.*		
3: *Mrs Birling acknowledges Mr Birling's commitment to his work.*	men with important work ... have to spend nearly all their time and energy on their business. you'll have to get used to that just as i did"	sheila is taught not to question social traditions or social heracnies

❹ Write up **point 1** into a **paragraph** below, in your own words:

In the beggining of the play the audience are shown that mr Birling is pleased that his daughter is marrying a Croft. The Birlings and Crofts marrying are more revolves around business than love, "we may look formard to the time when Crofts and Birlings are working togeter"

❺ Now, choose **one** of your **other points** and write it out as **another paragraph** here:

....

....

....

....

....

....

PROGRESS LOG [tick the correct box]   Needs more work ☐   Getting there ☐   Under control ☐

Practice task

❶ First, **read** this **exam-style** task:

Question: Choose three characters from *An Inspector Calls* and describe their attitude to responsibility.

❷ Begin by circling the **key words** in the **question** above.

❸ Now, complete this table, noting down **3–4 key points** with **evidence** and the **effect** created:

Point	Evidence/quotation	Meaning or effect

❹ **Draft your response**. Use the space below for your first paragraph(s) and then continue onto a sheet of paper.

Start: *The three characters I wish to focus on all show different attitudes to responsibility. For example …*

....

....

....

....

....

....

....

....

....

....

....

....

....

....

PROGRESS LOG [tick the correct box]   Needs more work ☐   Getting there ☐   Under control ☐

PART FIVE: LANGUAGE AND STRUCTURE

Language

1 First **match** these **words/expressions** to their **meanings** without checking the play:

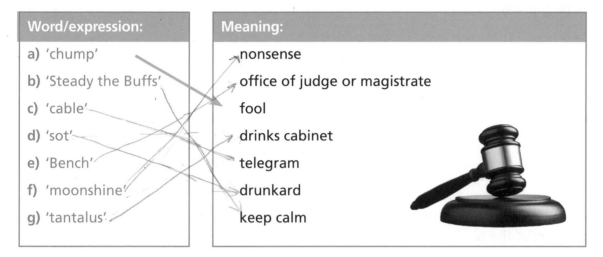

Word/expression:	Meaning:
a) 'chump'	nonsense
b) 'Steady the Buffs'	office of judge or magistrate
c) 'cable'	fool
d) 'sot'	drinks cabinet
e) 'Bench'	telegram
f) 'moonshine'	drunkard
g) 'tantalus'	keep calm

2 Now check the **words in context**. Look at the following pages. Do you want to change any of your answers?

a) p. 5; **b)** p. 5; **c)** p. 4; **d)** p. 35; **e)** p. 10; **f)** p. 70; **g)** p. 25

THINKING MORE DEEPLY

3 For each of the **feelings** listed below, think of a moment in the play when it is expressed. Find a **quotation** to back up each of your examples:

Feeling	Moment in the play	Quotation
1: Sadness	*When Gerald is overcome at the knowledge that Eva Smith/Daisy Renton is dead*	
2: Panic		
3: Happiness		

4 Now **underline** the **key words** in each quotation that convey the **feeling**.

❺ Read these comments from Sheila as she hears the account of Gerald's affair. From the list below choose the best **adjective** to sum up the **tone** of each comment:

a) 'So that's what you think I'm really like. I'm glad I realized' (Act Two, p. 28) ....

b) 'It's no use Gerald. You're wasting time.' (Act Two, p. 33) ....

c) 'the wonderful Fairy Prince. You must have adored it, Gerald.' (Act Two, p. 38) ....

d) 'Go on, Gerald. You went down into the bar, which is a favourite haunt of women of the town.' (Act Two, p. 34) ....

despairing	*sad*	*frank*	*sarcastic*	*cold*
angry	*impatient*	*serious*	*bitter*	

❻ Write a **sentence** to describe how Sheila's **tone of voice** has changed towards Gerald since the start of the play:

....

....

In the play several **literary techniques** are used (of which the most important is dramatic irony). Read the **definitions** of these literary techniques:

Dramatic irony – when the audience or a character knows something that the other characters don't

Symbolism – something that represents a big idea or quality (for example, a dove represents peace)

Euphemism – a word or phrase used in place of a harsher one that usually means something unpleasant

❼ Complete the table below, identifying the **technique** used in each example/ quotation and giving the **meaning or effect**:

Example or quotation	Literary technique	Meaning/effect
1: *The Inspector*	*Symbolism*	*He is the symbol of conscience, of our need to consider the welfare of others.*
2: 'And one day, I hope, Eric, when you've a daughter of your own' (Act One, p. 4)		
3: 'the girl's condition' (Act Three, p. 53)		

EXAM PREPARATION: WRITING ABOUT THE INSPECTOR'S FINAL SPEECH

Re-read the Inspector's speech (Act Three, p. 56) beginning *'Inspector: But just remember this.'* to *'Good night.'*

Question: What techniques does J. B. Priestley use to accentuate the Inspector's message?

Think about:

- How he delivers his speech
- The effect he has on the other characters

8 Complete this table:

Technique	Example	Effect
1: *Repetition*	*'**We** don't live alone. **We** are members of one body. **We** are responsible for each other.'*	*Stresses key words. The pronoun 'we' emphasises our shared responsibility*
2: *Long and short sentences in succession*		
3: *Metaphor*		

9 Write up **point 1** into a **paragraph** below, in your own words:

....
....
....
....
....
....

10 Now, choose **one** of your **other points** and write it out as **another paragraph** here:

....
....
....
....
....
....

PROGRESS LOG [tick the correct box]   Needs more work ☐   Getting there ☐   Under control ☐

Structure

QUICK TEST

❶ Without checking the play, try to remember in which **Act** each of these scenes takes place:

Scene	Act
1: The Inspector questions Mrs Birling	
2: Mr Birling rings Colonel Roberts	
3: The Inspector arrives	
4: The Inspector's final speech	
5: Gerald leaves the stage after he's been questioned	
4: We learn that Eric has stolen money	

THINKING MORE DEEPLY

❷ Write **one** or **two sentences** in response to each of these questions about the **structure** and **plot**:

a) How does J. B. Priestley build tension at the end of Act One and why?

....

....

....

b) What *two* important twists occur in Act Three?

....

....

....

....

c) How does the Inspector control the action of the play?

....

....

....

PROGRESS LOG [tick the correct box]　　Needs more work ☐　　Getting there ☐　　Under control ☐

Practice task

❶ First, **read** this **exam-style** task:

Read the stage directions at the beginning of Act One.

Question: How do the stage directions tell us that the play was not set in modern times?

❷ Begin by circling the **key words** in the **question** above.

❸ Now, complete this table, noting down **3–4 key points** with **evidence** and the **effect** created:

Point	Evidence/quotation	Meaning or effect

❹ **Draft your response.** Use the space below for your first paragraph(s) and then continue onto a sheet of paper.

Start: *In the stage directions, there are several details that tell us the play was not set in modern times. Firstly,* ....

....

....

....

....

....

....

....

....

....

....

....

PROGRESS LOG [tick the correct box]   Needs more work ☐   Getting there ☐   Under control ☐

PART SIX: GRADE BOOSTER

Writing skills

1 How well can you express your ideas about *An Inspector Calls*? Look at this grid and tick the level you think you are currently at:

Level	How you respond	What your spelling, punctuation and grammar is like	Tick
Higher	• You analyse the effect of specific words and phrases very closely (i.e. 'zooming in' on them and exploring their meaning). • You select quotations very carefully and you embed them fluently in your sentences. • You are persuasive and convincing in the points you make, often coming up with original ideas.	• You use a wide range of specialist terms (words like 'imagery'), excellent punctuation, accurate spelling, grammar, etc.	
Mid	• You analyse some parts of the text closely, but not all the time. • You support what you say with evidence and quotations, but sometimes your writing could be more fluent to read. • You make relevant comments on the text.	• You use a good range of specialist terms, generally accurate punctuation, spelling, grammar, etc.	
Lower	• You comment on some words and phrases but often you do not develop your ideas. • You sometimes use quotations to back up what you say but they are not always well chosen. • You mention the effect of certain words and phrases but these are not always relevant to the task.	• You do not have a very wide range of specialist terms, but you use reasonably accurate spellings, punctuation and grammar.	

SELECTING AND USING QUOTATIONS

2 Read these two samples from students' responses to a question about Eric. Decide which of the three levels they fit best, i.e. **lower** (L), **mid** (M) or **higher** (H).

Student A: *Eric is rude when Sheila and Gerald are talking. We are told he 'suddenly guffaws'. He cannot say why he laughed and Sheila thinks he is drunk. She says he is 'squiffy'. Both his laughter and drinking makes us think Eric is nervous when he is with other people.*

Level ? ☐ Why? ....

....

Student B: *J. B. Priestley demonstrates Eric's immaturity when he 'suddenly guffaws' at the dinner table while Sheila and Gerald are celebrating their engagement. Eric's inability to explain why he laughed leads Sheila to believe that he is 'squiffy', or slightly drunk, and we can further deduce Eric is ill at ease in company on important occasions.*

Level ? ☐ Why? ....

....

ZOOMING IN – YOUR TURN!

Here is the first part of another student response. The student has picked a good quotation but hasn't 'zoomed in' on any particular words or phrases:

When the Birlings begin to question whether or not Inspector Goole was a real police Inspector, Eric comments, 'He was our police inspector all right,' which reveals that Eric can be sardonic.

❸ Pick out one of the **words** or **phrases** the student has quoted and write a further sentence to complete the explanation:

The word/phrase '...............................' suggests that ....

....

....

EXPLAINING IDEAS

You need to be precise about the way J. B. Priestley gets ideas across. This can be done by varying your use of verbs (not just using 'says' or 'means').

❹ Read this paragraph from a **mid-level** response to a question about Eric's relationship with his father. Circle all the **verbs** that are repeated:

Priestley shows us the depth of Eric's misery when he accuses Mr Birling of not being 'the kind of father a chap could go to when he's in trouble'. It not only says that there is little trust between the two, and shows a father to whom Eric cannot admit weakness, it also says Mr Birling is an unsympathetic man.

❺ Now choose some of the words in the bank below to replace your circled ones:

suggests	*implies*	*tells us*	*presents*	*signals*	*asks*
demonstrates	*recognise*	*comprehends*	*reveals*	*conveys*	

❻ Rewrite your **higher-level** version of the paragraph in full below. Remember to mention the **author by name** to show you understand he is **making choices** in how he presents characters, themes and events.

....

....

....

....

....

....

....

PROGRESS LOG [tick the correct box]   Needs more work ☐   Getting there ☐   Under control ☐

Spelling, punctuation and grammar

Here are a number of key words you might use when writing in the exam:

Content and structure	Characters and style	Linguistic features
Act	character	metaphor
scene	role	personification
quotation	protagonist	juxtaposition
sequence	dramatic	dramatic irony
dialogue	tragedy	repetition
climax	villainous	symbol
development	humorous	monologue
stage directions	sympathetic	euphemism

1 Circle any you might find difficult to spell, and then use the 'Look, Say, Cover, Write, Check' method to learn them. This means: **look** at the word; **say** it out loud; then **cover** it up; **write** it out (without looking at it!); uncover and **check** your spelling with the correct version.

2 Create a **mnemonic** for five of your difficult spellings. For example,

tragedy: **t**en **r**eally **a**ngry **g**irls **e**njoyed **d**ancing **y**esterday!   Or …

break the word down: T – RAGE – DY!

a) ....

b) ....

c) ....

d) ....

e) ....

3 Circle any **incorrect spellings** in this paragraph and then rewrite it:

At the end of Act Two, the tention builds dramataically as Mrs Birling, 'exchainges a frightened glance with her husband', and they relise that Eric has been involved with Eva Smith. By the time the curtain falls, J. B. Priestley ensures that the audiense knows that Eric is the likely father of Eva Smith's unborn child.

....

....

....

....

....

....

....

④ **Punctuation** can help make your meaning clear. Here is one response by a student commenting on Priestley's choice of the name 'Goole' for the Inspector. Check for correct use of:

● Apostrophes, full stops, commas and capital letters

● Speech marks for quotations and emphasis

When Priestley gives the Inspector the name of 'Goole', we think of the word 'ghoul' which is another word for 'ghost' or phantom since the Inspector is a mysterious figure and as Gerald discovers, 'in act three wasn't a police officer', the name 'Goole' may well have been Priestleys special choice.

Rewrite it **correctly** here:

....

....

....

....

....

....

⑤ It is better to use the **present tense** to describe what is happening in the play.

Look at these two extracts. Which one uses tenses **consistently** and **accurately**?

Student A: *Priestley told us through the powerful character of the Inspector that 'we are responsible for each other', and so emphasised the importance of community. This view is opposite to that of Mr Birling who believed that, 'a man has to look after himself... and his family'.*

Student B: *Priestley tells us through the powerful character of the Inspector that 'we are responsible for each other', and so emphasises the importance of community. This view is opposite to that of Mr Birling who believes that, 'a man has to look after himself... and his family'.*

⑥ Now look at this further paragraph. Underline or circle all the verb **tenses** first.

Sheila <u>tried</u> to make her mother understand that she had been building, 'a kind of wall' between the family 'and that girl', Eva Smith. The word 'wall' was an image Priestley used to imply a barrier that Mrs Birling was constructing to protect herself from admitting the truth.

Now rewrite it using the **present tense** consistently:

....

....

....

....

....

....

PROGRESS LOG [tick the correct box]   Needs more work ☐   Getting there ☐   Under control ☐

Planning and structure

STRUCTURE AND LINKING OF PARAGRAPHS

❶ Read this **paragraph** by a student who is explaining how J. B. Priestley presents Mr Birling:

We know about Mr Birling when he says to Gerald, 'I speak as a hard-headed business man who has to take risks'. This tells us that he is a tough businessman and takes chances.

Expert viewpoint: This paragraph is unclear. It does not begin with a topic sentence to explain how Priestley presents Mr Birling and doesn't zoom in on any key words that tell us what Mr Birling is like.

Now **rewrite the paragraph in your own words**. Start with a **topic sentence**, and pick out a **key word or phrase** to **'zoom in'** on:

J. B. Priestley presents Mr Birling as ....

....

....

....

....

....

❷ Read this **paragraph** by another student also commenting on how Mr Birling is presented:

Priestley gives us a vivid picture of Mr Birling. This can be found in the initial stage directions. He describes him as, 'a heavy-looking, rather portentous man in his middle fifties'. This gives the impression that he is solid and practical. It suggests a no-nonsense kind of person. He is also an older man. The description also tells us he is pompous.

Expert viewpoint: The candidate has understood how the character's nature is revealed in his appearance. However, the paragraph is rather awkwardly written. It needs improving by linking the sentences with suitable phrases and joining words such as: 'where', 'in', 'as well as', 'who', 'suggesting', 'implying'.

Rewrite the **paragraph**, improving the **style**, and also try to add a **concluding sentence** summing up Mr Birling's appearance.

Start with the same **topic sentence**, but extend it:

Priestley gives us a vivid picture of Mr Birling ....

....

....

....

....

....

....

PLANNING AN ESSAY

❸ Read this **exam-style** task:

Question: *How does J. B. Priestley depict the relationship between workers and employers in the play?*

Select the **key words** in this question by **underlining or highlighting** them. The first has been done for you.

❹ Write a simple **plan** with **five key points** (the first two have been done for you). Think about the Birlings, Gerald, who holds power and who is affected.

a) *Priestley depicts Mrs Birling's disdainful attitude to servants.*

b) *He depicts Mr Birling's intolerant attitude to his workforce.*

c) ....

....

d) ....

....

e) ....

....

❺ Now list **five quotations**, one for each point (the first two have been provided for you):

a) *'Birling: …Good dinner too, Sybil. Tell cook from me' 'Mrs Birling: (reproachfully) Arthur, you're not supposed to say such things –'*

b) *'Birling: … labour trouble …. Don't worry. … We employers at last are coming together to see that our interests … are properly protected.'*

c) ....

....

d) ....

....

e) ....

....

❻ Now read this task and **write a plan of your own**, including **quotations**, on a separate sheet of paper.

Read from the stage directions *'The INSPECTOR enters and EDNA goes'* (Act One, p. 11) to the stage directions *'and now BIRLING notices him.'* (Act One, p. 13).

Question: *How is the Inspector depicted in this scene and how does Mr Birling respond to him?*

PROGRESS LOG [tick the correct box]   Needs more work ☐   Getting there ☐   Under control ☐

Sample answers

OPENING PARAGRAPHS

Here is one of the tasks from the previous page:

Question: *How does J. B. Priestley depict the relationship between workers and employers in the play?*

Now look at these two alternate openings to the essay and read the expert viewpoints underneath:

Student A

> *Priestley depicts the relationship between workers and employers in several different ways and circumstances. As the play opens, we see how Edna the Birlings' maid behaves and is treated and the cook is also mentioned. Later we see how Mr Birling treats his workers at the factory, including Eva Smith in particular, as well as the effect Sheila Birling has on her.*

Student B

> *Mr Birling treats his workers badly. They work for him in his factory but he does not want to pay them an increase. So they go on strike. That means Mr Birling sacks the ring leaders without thinking about them. One of these is Eva Smith. So she has to get another job.*

Expert viewpoint 1: This is a clear opening paragraph that outlines some of the relationships to be discussed. It also suggests that these relationships take place in different settings and circumstances. How Sheila affects Eva Smith through Eva's employers, Milwards, should have been mentioned more fully.

Expert viewpoint 2: This opening recounts the relationship between Mr Birling and his workers, without outlining what is to be discussed in the essay, which is the point of the introduction. Other kinds of worker/employer relationships need to be mentioned.

❶ Which comment belongs to which answer? Match the paragraph (A or B) to the expert's feedback (1 or 2).

Student A: .... Student B: ....

❷ Now it's your turn. Write the opening paragraph to this task on a separate sheet of paper:

Read from the stage directions *'The INSPECTOR enters and EDNA goes'* (Act One, p. 11) to the stage directions *'and now BIRLING notices him.'* (Act One, p. 13).

Question: *How is the Inspector depicted in this scene and how does Mr Birling respond to him?*

Remember:

- Introduce the topic in general terms, perhaps **explaining** or **'unpicking'** the key **words** or **ideas** in the task (such as 'depict').

- Mention the **different possibilities** or ideas that you are going to address.

- Use the **author's name**.

WRITING ABOUT TECHNIQUES

Here are two paragraphs in response to a different task, where the students have focused on the writer's techniques. The task is:

Read from *'Birling: (jovially) But the whole thing's different now'* (p. 70) to the stage directions *'the curtain falls.'* (p. 72).

Question: *What techniques does Priestley use to show the impact of the Inspector's words in this scene?*

Student A

> *When Sheila repeats the Inspector's words she says, 'Fire and blood and anguish.' This tells us that she is afraid about the future if people do not help one another or there is no community spirit. The way Priestley chooses to repeat the words through another character drives home his message to the audience. And as we know there was trouble in the future.*

Student B

> *Priestley chooses Sheila to repeat the Inspector's powerful words, 'Fire and blood and anguish,' so conveying her fears for future conflict if we do not care for one another. Not only has the Inspector had a profound effect on Sheila, but also the repetition of these words particularly from the mouth of a member of the wealthy class, reinforces Priestley's message that conflict will certainly occur. Ironically, we know it did, both in the conflict of two World Wars and the General Strike of 1926, when there was wide-scale industrial action.*

Expert viewpoint 1: This higher-level response describes the impact that the Inspector's words had on Sheila. It also states the wider implications of the Inspector's words for the audience and gives evidence. It discusses the writer's techniques, using literary terms to good effect. The second sentence is a little long, but nonetheless links ideas very successfully.

Expert viewpoint 2: This mid-level response highlights the effect of the Inspector's words on Sheila. However, the quotation, though appropriate, is not sufficiently embedded in the sentence. There is one instance of the writer's technique mentioned but no others and in the final sentence the point made is not developed and no evidence or examples are given.

❸ Which comment belongs to which answer? Match the paragraph (A or B) to the expert's feedback (1 or 2).

Student A: .... **Student B:** ....

❹ Now, take another **aspect** of the scene and on a separate sheet of paper write your own **paragraph**. You could **comment** on one of these aspects:

● Mr Birling's response at the beginning of the scene

● The changes of mood throughout the scene

● The end of the play

Now read this **lower-level** response to the following task:

Read from the stage directions *'The INSPECTOR enters and EDNA goes'* (Act One, p. 11) to the stage directions *'and now Birling notices him.'* (Act One, p. 13).

Question: *How is the Inspector depicted in this scene and how does Mr Birling respond to him?*

Student response

> When Edna the maid leaves the Inspector stands there, *'he creates at once an impression of massiveness, solidity and purposefulness.'* This means he looks big and means business. He also has a habit of staring at people hard so that they get worried. He is not bothered by any of the other characters and they have never met him before.
>
> The Inspector does not want a drink from Mr Birling. He wants to know if Mr Birling knows about Eva Smith and he asks questions. He has a photo that he shows Mr Birling, but he does not show it to the others because he wants to get on and do things his way.

Expert viewpoint: The quotation in paragraph one is well chosen and gives us a sense of the Inspector's presence, but there is no attempt to embed it in a sentence. Nor is there any exploration in either paragraph of the effect the Inspector has on Mr Birling and how he responds. Comments on what Priestley intends in this scene are needed, and the language the student uses is sometimes too informal, as in, 'means business'.

⑤ **Rewrite** these two **paragraphs** in your own words, improving them by addressing:

- The lack of development of linking of points – no **'zooming in'** on **key words and phrases**

- The lack of **quotations and embedding**

- Unnecessary **repetition**, and poor use of **specialist terms** and **vocabulary**

Paragraph 1:

In this scene, Priestley depicts the Inspector as ....

....

and also ....

....

This implies that ....

....

Paragraph 2:

Mr Birling's response to the Inspector is at first ....

....

However ....

....

This links to ....

....

A FULL-LENGTH RESPONSE

⑥ Write a full-length response to this exam-style task on a separate sheet of paper. Answer both parts of the question:

Read from *'Birling: (somewhat impatiently) Look – there's nothing mysterious'* (Act One, p. 13) to *'Inspector: … But after all it's better to ask for the earth than to take it.'* (Act One, p. 15).

Part A

How does J. B. Priestley depict Eva Smith in this scene?

Part B

How does J. B. Priestley show the effect the Inspector has on the main characters by the end of the play?

- Plan **quickly** (no more than 5 minutes) what you intend to write, jotting down **4 or 5 supporting quotations**.

- Refer closely to the **key words** in the question.

- Make sure you comment on **what** the writer does, the **techniques** he uses and the **effect** of those techniques.

- Support your points with **well-chosen quotations** or other evidence.

- Develop your points by **'zooming in'** on particular **words** or **phrases** and explaining their **effect**.

- Be **persuasive** and **convincing** in what you say.

- Carefully check your **spelling, punctuation** and **grammar**.

PROGRESS LOG [tick the correct box]   Needs more work ☐   Getting there ☐   Under control ☐

Further questions

1. What do you think J. B. Priestley intended when he created the character of the Inspector?

2. Which character do you think has changed least by the end of the play and why?

3. What indications are there that Sheila and Gerald have a future together and from the evidence in the play what would that be like and why?

4. The structure of the play is carefully worked out. What part does the Inspector play in this?

5. There are several themes in the play, such as equality and responsibility. What do you think is the most important theme and why? (You can write about a theme not mentioned.)

PROGRESS LOG [tick the correct box]   Needs more work ☐   Getting there ☐   Under control ☐

ANSWERS

NOTE: Answers have been provided for most tasks. Exceptions are 'Practice tasks' and tasks which ask you to write a paragraph or use your own words or judgement.

PART ONE: INTRODUCTION [pp. 6–7]

1 Setting: The Birlings' House: All characters (except Eva Smith/Daisy Renton). The entire play is set here. **The Police Station:** The Inspector. **The Factory:** Where Mr Birling runs his business, Eric Birling works and Eva Smith worked. **Milwards:** Where Sheila Birling shops and Eva Smith worked. **Palace Variety Theatre:** Where Gerald Croft and Eric Birling met Eva Smith/Daisy Renton. **Hospital/Mortuary:** Where the body of Eva Smith was taken.

2 Characters: Who's who: Mrs Birling, Inspector Goole, Eva Smith/ Daisy Renton, Gerald Croft, Mr Birling, Eric Birling, Sheila Birling

3 J. B. Priestley: Author and context: a) 1906; b) France; c) Cambridge; d) *Diversions*; e) 1926; f) 1929; g) *Journey*; h) talks; i) 1945

PART TWO: PLOT AND ACTION [pp. 8–37]

Act One, Part 1: The dinner party [pp. 8–9]

1 a) F; b) F; c) T; d) T; e) T; f) F; g) F

2 a) The Birlings are wealthy, prosperous business people. Their daughter is engaged to the son of a lord.

b) Their relationship is affectionate and caring but overshadowed by doubts about Gerald's commitment to Sheila.

c) We learn that Eric drinks too much. He is shy and awkward in company, but can be out-spoken.

3

Point/detail	Evidence	Effect or explanation
1: He believes the powerful and wealthy should protect their position.	'We employers at last are coming together to see our interests … are properly protected.'	His comments imply that he disregards the workforce he employs.
2: He likes to speak at length and expects to be listened to.	He make statements such as: 'Now you three young people, just listen to this – and remember what I'm telling you now.'	He has a high opinion of himself and regards himself as a person of authority.
3: He is confident that future technology will bring prosperity.	He claims that, 'The world's developing so fast that it'll make war impossible.'	He does not take into account other points of view and this clouds his judgement.

Act One, Part 2: Mr Birling confides in Gerald [pp. 10–11]

1 a) Lord Mayor; b) knighthood; c) possible scandal; d) clothes; e) claims not to remember something

2 a) Mr Birling understands why Lady Croft might prefer Gerald to marry from within his own class. He uses the possibility of a knighthood to impress Gerald and, through him, Lady Croft.

b) Gerald shares confidences with Mr Birling and compliments him. They share a joke at Eric's expense.

c) Eric is uneasy, and feels excluded from Gerald and his father. He finds it difficult to take a joke.

3

Point/detail	Evidence	Effect or explanation
1: He believes he will be knighted (for contributions to the community).	'I've always been regarded as a sound useful party man.'	His comments suggest that a knighthood will depend on his support for the right people and political party.
2: He believes in self reliance.	He says, 'a man has to mind his own business and look after himself and his own'.	This reveals he feels no responsibility for others in the wider community.
3: He has no respect for the community.	He comments, 'you'd think everybody has to look after everybody else … community and all that nonsense.'	This reveals his hypocrisy. He is happy to receive an honour from the community while believing the community to be worthless.

Act One, Part 3: The enquiry begins [pp. 12–13]

1 We first meet Inspector **Goole** when Edna, the maid, announces him. Although not a **big/large** man, he is an imposing figure. Mr Birling tries to impress the Inspector by pointing out that he was an alderman and also Lord Mayor and still sits on the **Bench**, meaning he is a magistrate. The Inspector explains that a girl died in the Infirmary after swallowing strong **disinfectant**. A letter and a diary were found in her room. She had more than one name, but her original name was **Eva Smith** and she worked at Mr Birling's **factory/works**. The Inspector shows Mr Birling a **photograph** of the girl. Eventually Mr Birling remembers that he sacked her because of her part in a **strike** for higher wages.

2 a) Mr Birling wanted to emphasise his importance in the community. He wanted to try to take charge when the Inspector arrived.

b) Gerald agrees with Mr Birling that there was no choice but to sack her. He thinks strictness with the workforce is important.

c) A 'chain of events' is when one event leads to another and each action has a reaction or consequence.

3

Point/detail	Evidence	Effect or explanation
1: Mr Birling cares about the profit his company makes.	'it's my duty to keep labour costs down'.	His comments tell us that he values the profit he makes more than a good wage for his workers.
2: Eric is sympathetic to the hardship Eva Smith faced.	He says: 'He could have kept her [Eva Smith] on instead of throwing her out.'	Eric shows greater concern for people than money.
3: We can further compare Mr Birling and Eric's points of view about taking responsibility for the workers.	'Mr Birling: … if they [his workers] didn't like those rates, they could go and work somewhere else. It's a free country … 'Eric: It isn't if you can't go and work somewhere else.'	Mr Birling feels no responsibility for what happens to his workers, while Eric does.

Act One, Part 4: Sheila's sympathy turns to shock [pp. 14–15]

1 a) the Inspector; b) Eva Smith; c) Eva Smith; d) Sheila, Eric and Gerald know something about Eva Smith; e) factory workers; f) Sheila recognised Eva Smith; g) the Inspector upsetting Sheila

2 a) The Inspector describes in detail the agony of Eva Smith's death. He emphasises how attractive she was and her potential.

b) Mr Birling becomes less assertive and more reasonable in tone. He fears a scandal.

c) The Inspector shows the photograph to one character at a time so that none of the characters know whether or not they have seen the same photograph. This also creates mystery around both Eva Smith and the Inspector.

3

Point/detail	Evidence	Effect or explanation
1: *Sheila scolds her father for sacking Eva Smith.*	*'I think it was a mean thing to do. Perhaps that spoilt everything for her.'*	*She not only feels sympathy for Eva Smith but also recognises the possible consequences of her father's actions.*
2: *Sheila begins to realise that Eva is the girl she had sacked from Milwards.*	*'Sheila: (staring at him, agitated) When was this?'*	*Sheila asks the Inspector when the sacking took place to confirm her suspicions that she was responsible. She is disturbed by what she is beginning to realise.*
3: *Sheila recognises the girl in the photograph the Inspector shows her.*	*The stage directions tell us: 'She looks at it closely, recognizes it with a little cry, gives a half-stifled sob, and then runs out.'*	*When she realises that the photo is of the shop assistant at Milwards, she realises her part in Eva Smith's downfall and is overcome.*

Act One, Part 5: Sheila and the shop girl [pp. 16–17]

1 a) T; b) F; c) T; d) F; e) F; f) T; g) T

2 a) Sheila was jealous of Eva Smith's attractiveness. She also has a bad temper.

b) Sheila reacts with horror and embarrassment at the consequences of her actions. She makes a promise never to treat someone like that again.

c) Sheila's questioning of Gerald about Daisy Renton adds drama to the end of Act One. She also suspects that the Inspector knows more and that there will be more questions to follow.

3

Point/detail	Evidence	Effect or explanation
1: *The Inspector deliberately refuses Gerald's request*	*'Gerald: I'd like to look at that photograph now, Inspector.* *'Inspector: All in good time.'*	*The Inspector is calm and increasingly in control of the situation.*
2: *He states his opinion regardless of whom he is speaking to.*	*'Gerald: … we're respectable citizens and not criminals.* *'Inspector: Sometimes … I wouldn't know where to draw the line.'*	*He is judgemental, challenging and authoritative.*

| 3: *He states the consequences of Eva Smith's dismissal from Milwards.* | *'Sheila: …Did it make much difference to her?*

 'Inspector: Yes, I'm afraid it did. … she decided she might as well try another kind of life.' | *The Inspector is stark and honest about Sheila's part in Eva Smith's downfall.* |

Act Two, Part 1: Sharing the guilt [pp. 18–19]

1 a) where Act One finished; b) in the doorway; c) laughs hysterically; d) quarrel; e) interrupts Gerald and Sheila; f) unaware of the situation; g) politely; h) does not understand Sheila

2 a) Gerald is afraid that Sheila will find out the details of his affair with Daisy Renton. He is also afraid that their relationship will end.

b) Mrs Birling claims they can't help the Inspector. She tries to make light of the situation.

c) Sheila tries to prevent her mother from being dismissive. She fears her mother's attitude will prove regrettable.

3

Point/detail	Evidence	Effect or explanation
1: *Sheila suspects that Gerald is also implicated in Eva Smith/Daisy Renton's death.*	*She says to the Inspector: 'you haven't finished asking questions – have you? … Then I'm staying.'*	*She wants to hear the truth, even if it is unpleasant.*
2: *But she still feels she is to blame.*	*'Inspector: And if she [Sheila] leaves us now, and doesn't hear any more, then she'll feel she's entirely to blame'*	*She could shoulder the guilt entirely, unless she listens to the Inspector's questions.*
3: *The Inspector discusses shared responsibility.*	*'Inspector: … we have to share something. If there's nothing else, we'll have to share our guilt.'*	*Sheila is affected by his words. She recognises that while she must share the blame she is not entirely responsible for Eva Smith's death.*

Act Two, Part 2: Mrs Birling bustles [pp. 20–1]

1 *Mrs Birling enters in a **confident/bold/self-assured** manner, which is very different to the mood of the others in the room. When Mrs Birling comments that the Inspector has made an impression on her **daughter/child**, he replies that this often happens with the young. Sheila is determined to stay, despite her mother's comment that Sheila has a morbid curiosity about the girl's **suicide/death**. As the scene develops, Mrs Birling's self-importance increases and she accuses the Inspector of being **impertinent/rude/cheeky**. She reminds him that **Mr Birling** was once Lord Mayor. However, she is shocked to learn of the seriousness of **Eric's** drinking habit.*

2 a) The first meaning of 'offence' is 'insult'. The second meaning is 'crime' (you could think about in what sense Eva Smith's death is a crime).

b) The Inspector questions Mrs Birling about Eric's drinking to make her face the seriousness of it. His questioning also suggests to us that his drinking may have a part to play later.

c) Gerald responds honestly, saying that Eric drinks a lot. He also responds sensitively and with regret.

ANSWERS

3

Point/detail	Evidence	Effect or explanation
1: Sheila is aware that Mrs Birling does not accept that the family may have played a part in Eva Smith's death.	'You mustn't try to build up a kind of wall between us and that girl.'	The 'wall' is a way in which Mrs Birling separates herself (and her family and Gerald) from possible guilt.
2: Sheila is warning her mother what will happen if she fails to answer the Inspector's questions.	'Sheila: ... the Inspector will just break it [the wall] down. And it'll be the worse when he does.'	The Inspector will break down Mrs Birling's defences and reveal her guilt.
3: Mrs Birling fails to understand.	'Sheila: But, Mother, do stop before it's too late. 'Mrs Birling: If you mean that the Inspector will take offence –'	Mrs Birling is more concerned about good manners than allowing the Inspector to question her.

Act Two, Part 3: Gerald's confession [pp. 22–3]

1 a) Eric; b) Sheila; c) Daisy Renton/Eva Smith; d) Gerald; e) Alderman Meggarty; f) Daisy Renton/Eva Smith and Gerald; g) Gerald

2 a) Gerald's confession gives us greater knowledge of Daisy Renton/Eva Smith. His confession also creates greater sympathy for him.

b) Sheila urges the characters not to be evasive; to come to the point. She also suggests the Inspector has foreknowledge.

c) Sheila returns her engagement ring to Gerald. She does, however, leave the way open for a renewal of the relationship.

3

Point/detail	Evidence	Effect or explanation
1: The Inspector asks simple questions.	He asks questions of Gerald such as: 'When did this affair end?'; 'How did she take it?'; 'She had to move out of those rooms?'	These questions, which often build on what the characters say, encourage the characters to reveal further events and actions.
2: Gerald is curious about the Inspector's knowledge.	'Gerald: How do you know that? 'Inspector: She kept a rough sort of diary. 'Gerald: (gravely) I see.'	The diary is a device that convinces characters (such as Gerald) of the Inspector's knowledge.
3: Gerald reacts to the information about Daisy Renton.	He says, 'I'm rather more – upset – by this business than I probably appear to be – and – well, I'd like to be alone for a while.'	Gerald accepts what the Inspector says and is greatly troubled by his description of Daisy's happy memory of the affair.

Act Two, Part 4: Sheila warns her mother [pp. 24–5]

1 a) F; b) T; c) T; d) F; e) F; f) F; g) T

2 a) Gerald expected the engagement to end. He does, however, want it to resume at some point.

b) Gerald does not see the photograph. Mrs Birling does see the photograph (but we cannot be sure it is the same one that was shown previously).

c) In this scene the Inspector demands answers. He also makes accusations (for example, of Mrs Birling).

3

Point/detail	Evidence	Effect or explanation
1: The Inspector demands the truth from Mrs Birling.	Mr Birling demands an apology but the Inspector counters: 'Apologize for what – doing my duty?'	The Inspector is not threatened by Mr Birling.
2: The Inspector reminds Mr Birling of his duties.	'Inspector: ... Public men, Mr Birling, have responsibilities as well as privileges.'	The Inspector takes a moral position, suggesting that Mr Birling lacks a sense of duty.
3: Sheila challenges her parents' haughtiness.	'Sheila: It means that we've no excuse for putting on airs ... Father threw this girl out'	She, unlike her parents, understands that the family have no claim to superiority because of the way they treated Eva Smith.

Act Two, Part 5: The deserving and the undeserving [pp. 26–7]

1 a) to say that Eric has left; b) over-excited; c) two weeks ago; d) refused to help Eva Smith; e) was chair of the committee; f) cruel; g) stolen money

2 a) Mrs Birling is prejudiced towards Eva Smith and feels she is impertinent to use the name 'Birling'. She sees Eva Smith as underserving of help and believes she lied.

b) Mr Birling is worried that the Press will find out about his wife's treatment of Eva Smith. He is concerned about a scandal.

c) Mrs Birling insists that the father of Eva Smith's child is responsible for her death. This creates a dramatic end to the Act, since we learn that Eric is the father.

3

Point/detail	Evidence	Effect or explanation
1: Eva Smith's name changes for a third time.	Mrs Birling says, 'First, she called herself Mrs Birling –'.	This implies that Eric (the only character left to be questioned) was involved with Eva.
2: Eva Smith was pregnant.	The Inspector says, 'It was because she [Eva] was going to have a child'.	The implication is that Eric was the father.
3: Sheila warns her mother not to insist that the father of Eva Smith's child should take responsibility.	She says, 'Mother – stop – stop!' 'Now, Mother – don't you see?'	Sheila guesses where the questions are leading and that Eric is the father.

Act Three, Part 1: Eric in the spotlight [pp. 28–9]

1 a) Mrs Birling to Eric; b) Eric to Mrs Birling; c) Mrs Birling to Eric; d) Eric to Sheila; e) Sheila to Eric; f) The Inspector to Eric; g) Eric to the Inspector

2 a) Eric's words mean that he is the father of Eva Smith's unborn child. He suspects that the other characters know this.

b) This shows that Mr Birling cares more about covering up the truth than finding it out.

c) Mrs Birling's mood changes when she discovers that Eric has taken sexual advantage of Eva Smith. She is then lead away, distressed.

3

Point/detail	Evidence	Effect or explanation
1: Eric had been drinking.	'I'd been there [in the Palace Bar] an hour or so with two or three chaps. I was a bit squiffy.'	His judgement would be impaired and his behaviour unstable.
2: He became increasingly drunk.	He says that at Eva Smith's lodgings, 'I was in that state when a chap easily turns nasty – and I threatened to make a row.'	He became hostile and aggressive.
3: He had sex with Eva Smith.	He says, 'And that's when it happened. And I didn't even remember – that's the hellish thing. Oh – my God!'	He treated her like a prostitute. Later he shows remorse.

Act Three, Part 2: A baby on the way [pp. 30–1]

1 Eric explains that he met Eva Smith again about **two** weeks later by accident at the **Palace Bar**. He says that they talked, and explains that he was not in love with her. **Mr Birling** is angry because Eric slept with Eva Smith again. The two men quarrel, but the **Inspector** intervenes in order to continue questioning **Eric**. Eric admits that when he discovered that Eva Smith was pregnant, he was worried about what would happen to him. He says that Eva Smith did not wish to **marry** him, and that he gave her money, about **fifty** pounds in total.

2 a) Eric had little regard for Eva Smith after their first meeting, and could not remember her name. He saw her as a passing fancy and did not arrange to meet again.

b) Eric insisted on giving Eva Smith money when he discovered she was pregnant.

c) Eric claims that Eva treated him as a child, which suggests immaturity. He is more worried about himself than Eva.

3

Point/detail	Evidence	Effect or explanation
1: Mr Birling uses language more freely in male company.	'So you had to go to bed with her?'	In 1912 a man like Mr Birling would not refer to sexual matters at all in front of women of his class.
2: The Inspector alters his language in male company.	He says, 'And you made love again?'	Despite his directness throughout the play, the Inspector also avoids referring to sex in female company.
3: We can compare Eric's earlier language with the language he uses in male company.	Earlier language: 'that's when it happened' In male company: 'fat old tarts'	The first quotation is a vague reference to the sexual act. The second refers to prostitutes, using language that Eric would never use in female company. The change of language suggests double standards.

Act Three, Part 3: 'Fire and blood and anguish' [pp. 32–3]

1 a) F; b) T; c) T; d) T; e) T; f) F; g) F

2 a) Mr Birling's main concern is that Eric has committed serious theft. He then starts to plan how to cover up the crime.

b) The Inspector connects the harsh deeds committed to show the characters' shared blame. He addresses each of the Birling family in turn.

c) In Act One the mood is happy and celebratory because of Sheila's engagement to Gerald. In Act Three the mood is one of fear and despair because of the revelations about Eva Smith.

3

Point/detail	Evidence	Effect or explanation
1: The Inspector reminds the Birlings that Eva Smith is dead and gone.	'You can't do her any more harm. And you can't do her any good now, either. You can't even say "I'm sorry, Eva Smith."'	It's too late to make amends to Eva Smith for the wrongs done to her.
2: He points out that there are others like Eva Smith.	'Inspector: ... but there are millions and millions and millions of Eva Smiths and John Smiths still left with us ... all intertwined with our lives'	He is pointing out that we have to be responsible for each other. He is making an appeal for a more caring, fairer society.
3: He warns of trouble for the future.	'Inspector: ... if men will not learn that lesson, then they will be taught it in fire and blood and anguish'	He is saying that without a fairer society there will be social unrest and conflict.

Act Three, Part 4: A lesson not learnt [pp. 34–5]

1 a) crying; b) pours himself a drink; c) get a knighthood; d) Eric; e) go to court; f) his sister; g) Gerald

2 a) Mr Birling turns on Eric because he believes he is the one most closely linked to Eva Smith's death. He also thinks Eric's behaviour will affect his own chances of a knighthood.

b) We are first alerted to the possibility that Inspector Goole may not be an inspector when Sheila asks at what point the Inspector arrived and questions whether he is a real inspector. The stage directions also tell us that Sheila is 'sharply attentive' and 'reflective'.

c) Sheila takes no comfort from the possibility that the Inspector is not a real one because, either way, a girl or girls were badly treated by the family. Whether or not Inspector Goole was a real inspector does not change what happened.

3

Point/detail	Evidence	Effect or explanation
1: Sheila is aware of the important consequences of what has happened.	'But now you're beginning all over again to pretend nothing much happened –'.	She points out to her father that he is still not facing his share of the blame for Eva Smith's death.
2: Mr Birling sees what has happened in a different light to Sheila.	He says, 'Nothing much happened! ... there'll be a public scandal ... and who here will suffer from that more than I will?'	Mr Birling sees what has happened only as a threat to his position.
3: Eric sarcastically reminds his father of his view that we should look after ourselves.	He says, 'You told us ... we weren't to take any notice of these cranks who tell us that everybody has to look after everybody else'.	We are being reminded of the Inspector's view, which has affected the younger but not the older generation.

ANSWERS

Act Three, Part 5: Three telephone calls [pp. 36–7]

1 a) Mr Birling about the Inspector; b) Gerald about the Inspector; c) Sheila about all the Birling family and Gerald; d) Mrs Birling about the Inspector; e) Mr Birling about Eric; f) Gerald about whether Eva Smith really died; g) Mrs Birling about Gerald

2 a) Gerald returns to bring news that Inspector Goole was not a police officer. He also comes back to make amends with Sheila.

b) Eric considers his mistreatment of Eva Smith to be his worst offence. By comparison, he says, stolen money is not important.

c) Mrs Birling seems to be most concerned that everyone shows good manners. She is particularly concerned that Sheila and Eric behave sensibly.

3

Point/detail	Evidence	Effect or explanation
1: Gerald establishes there was no recent suicide of any young girls.	'Mr Birling: (triumphantly) There you are! Proof positive: The whole story's just a lot of moonshine.'	The tension lessens. Mr Birling becomes buoyant and jovial at the news.
2: Sheila cannot forget that a girl (or girls) was badly treated, regardless of who she was.	'Sheila: … Everything we said had happened really had happened. If it didn't end tragically, then that's lucky for us. But it might have done.'	She remains troubled and despondent. She has taken to heart the events and the Inspector's message.
3: There is a final telephone call to say an inspector is on his way.	The stage directions read 'He [Mr Birling] puts the telephone down slowly and looks in a panic-stricken fashion at the others.'	His jovial mood quickly turns to one of shock.

PART THREE: CHARACTERS [pp. 39–45]

The Inspector [p. 39]

1

Quality	Moment/s in play	Quotation
a) Principled	He wants justice for Eva Smith and those like her.	'Inspector: We don't live alone … We are responsible for each other.'
b) Clever	He gets the characters to reveal their actions.	'Sheila: … Well, he inspected us all right.'
c) Inquiring	He feels he must reveal the truth.	'Inspector: It's my duty to ask questions.'
d) Mysterious	There is no record of an Inspector Goole.	'Gerald: There isn't any such inspector.'

2

'They are suddenly … at him.': *compelling* – shows the Inspector's magnetism

'This girl killed herself … *forget it.'*: *hard-hitting* language – he is tough

'You refused her …grant her.': *articulate* – shows he is skilful with words

Mr Birling [p. 40]

1, 2 successful p. 1; ambitious p. 8; talkative p. 7; business-like p. 6; self-important p. 59; cruel p. 71; selfish p. 58; dishonest p. 54; unjust p. 15; middle-aged p. 1; hard-headed p. 6

3 *Mr Birling regards himself as a man of **importance** who has achieved a public position, such as that of Lord **Mayor**. He is well-to-do, having made his money from **business/manufacturing** but has little time for those who **work** for him. His most important concern is to achieve a knighthood and he will do everything he can to prevent a **scandal** from spoiling his chances. Mr Birling feels no remorse for **sacking/dismissing** Eva Smith. He is not affected by the words of the Inspector and when he discovers that the Inspector may not be what he seems, he even **jokes** about the events surrounding the possible **death/suicide** of Eva Smith.*

Mrs Birling [p. 41]

1

Quality	Moment/s in play	Quotation
a) Cold	Stage directions at start of Act One	'a rather cold woman'
b) Prejudiced	When the Inspector challenges Mrs Birling about Eva Smith's claim	'You admit being prejudiced against her case?'
c) Unashamed	When Mrs Birling states she didn't believe Eva Smith, so didn't regret her actions	'you're quite wrong to suppose I shall regret what I did.'
d) Puritanical	When she discovers Gerald's affair with Daisy Renton/Eva Smith	'I don't think we want any further details of this disgusting affair'

2

'any pressure … quite mistaken.': *forceful* – she is domineering

'I used my … it refused.': *powerful* – she can control others' lives

'So … I prefer … any further': *abrupt* – she is blunt and direct

Sheila Birling [p. 42]

1 a) F; b) F; c) T; d) T; e) NEE; f) NEE; g) F

2 a) Sheila is in a happy mood at the beginning of the play because she is 'very pleased with life', having just got engaged to Gerald.

b) When she first meets the Inspector she realises that something is amiss when she hears her father's tone towards the Inspector.

c) Sheila is greatly affected by the Inspector's news, for example when she hears that Eva Smith died, 'so horribly' by drinking disinfectant.

d) Of all the characters, Sheila changes the most and she is the one who recognises the Inspector's message that 'We are responsible for each other'.

e) By the end of the play Sheila's relationship with Gerald has ended, and she is going to consider whether they have a future together.

Eric Birling [p. 43]

1

His background, age and manner	1: middle-class son of Mr and Mrs Birling, early twenties
	2 ill-at-ease, shy, but can also be outspoken, misfit
His behaviour and what he says or others say about him	1: drinks too much
	2: pleasure seeking, immature, looks for the easy option
His relationships	1: poor relationship with his father, who thinks Eric has too easy a life, especially when Eric steals money
	2: uncaring and nasty with Eva Smith at first, but develops a sense of responsibility for her and her unborn child

3

Evidence	Quotation
a) Eric is affected by what the Birlings did to Eva Smith.	'Eric: (shouting) And I say the girl's dead and we all helped to kill her – and that's what matters –'
b) Eric is affected by Eva Smith's courage.	'Eric: … She came to you [Mrs Birling] to protect me'
c) Eric despises his father's views.	'Eric: … You told us … we weren't to take any notice of these cranks … then one of those cranks walked in – the Inspector.'
d) Eric agrees with Sheila that their parents are ignoring the Inspector's words.	'Sheila: [to Mr Birling] … You began to learn something. And now you've stopped. … 'Eric: 'And I agree with Sheila.'

Gerald Croft [p. 44]

1, 2

easy-going p. 2; clever p. 62; two-timing p. 34; deceitful p. 33; discreet p. 36; business-minded p. 6; high-handed p. 36; polite p. 2; caring p. 35; mature p. 2; opportunistic p. 34; controlled p. 39

3 Gerald Croft belongs to the upper **class** since his parents are Lord and Lady Croft. At the beginning of the play he is **engaged** to Sheila Birling. **Mr Birling** considers Gerald to be a good catch not only because of his social position but also because he has a head for **business** like himself. When Sheila discovers Gerald's affair with **Daisy Renton** she is angry, but gives him credit for **admitting** to the relationship. Gerald was genuinely fond of the young girl and is **upset** by her death. By the end of the play he hopes that **Sheila** will take him back.

Eva Smith/Daisy Renton [p. 45]

1 a) NEE; b) T; c) T; d) F; e) T; f) NEE; g) F

2 a) We never meet the girl who was called Eva Smith or Daisy Renton because the Inspector holds the information on her (them) and we do not know if this is reliable.

b) However, we do know that a young girl (or girls) was badly treated by the Birling family and Gerald Croft.

c) For example, Mr Birling sacked a young girl from his factory, as one of 'four or five ring-leaders' demanding higher wages.

d) Gerald also knew the girl, called Daisy Renton, and had an affair with her.

e) For J. B. Priestley, the girl represents the workers of the time, the 'millions and millions and millions of Eva Smiths and John Smiths', who were exploited by the wealthy and those with power.

PART FOUR: KEY CONTEXTS AND THEMES [pp. 47–9]

Key contexts [p. 47]

1 a) Brumley; b) prosperous; c) in lodgings; d) takes place in the Birlings' home; e) caters for the rich; f) before the First World War

2 a) We know that the Birlings see themselves as superior because the parlourmaid, Edna, addresses Mrs Birling as 'Ma'am'. Mrs Birling also reproaches Mr Birling for mentioning the cook in company.

b) Mr Birling's workers wanted better pay. They went on strike and, as a result, the ringleaders, including Eva Smith, were sacked.

c) Milwards would be afraid to offend their wealthy customers. It would be easier to sack a worker than to offend valuable customers.

Key themes [pp. 48–9]

1 J. B. Priestley uses the Inspector as a way of showing how the **poor/ workers** in society are badly treated. He contrasts the easy, **affluent/ comfortable** life of the Birlings with workers such as Eva Smith who struggle to survive, particularly when **employment/work** is hard to get.

The Inspector's message about our **responsibility** to each other has little success with either **Mr Birling** or **Mrs Birling**. However, his message affects **Eric** who feels guilt and the need to change his behaviour. Sheila also accepts her guilt and the wider view that our lives are all **entwined/interdependent/linked**.

2 a) Sheila learns the importance of trust in a relationship. By the end of the play she is no longer sure that she knows or loves Gerald.

b) Eric and Gerald were both physically attracted to Eva Smith. They both used Eva Smith for their own pleasure, without any commitment to her.

c) The audience may have had a sense of history repeating itself. The second telephone call reinforces the idea of events being repeated.

3

Point/detail	Evidence	Effect or explanation
1: Mr Birling is pleased that his family and the Crofts will unite in marriage.	'we may look forward to the time when Crofts and Birlings … are working together — for lower costs and higher prices.'	His hopes for Sheila's marriage are largely to do with the marriage of the two businesses.
2: Mrs Birling comes from a higher class than her husband.	Stage directions: 'her husband's social superior'	Mr Birling's marriage helped to raise his social standing.
3: Mrs Birling acknowledges Mr Birling's commitment to his work.	'men with important work to do sometimes have to spend nearly all their time and energy on their business.'	Mrs Birling unwittingly suggests that Mr Birling's work matters more than his marriage and family.

PART FIVE: LANGUAGE AND STRUCTURE [pp. 51–4]

Language [pp. 51–3]

1 a) Chump/fool; b) Steady the Buffs/keep calm; c) cable/telegram; d) sot/drunkard; e) Bench/office of judge or magistrate; f) moonshine/ nonsense; g) tantalus/drinks cabinet

3, 4

Feeling	Moment in the play	Quotation
1: Sadness	When Gerald is overcome at the knowledge that Eva Smith/Daisy Renton is dead	'Sorry – I – well, I've <u>suddenly realized</u> – taken it in properly – that she's <u>dead</u>'
2: Panic	When Sheila realises the Inspector knows about Gerald's affair and more	'(laughs rather hysterically) Why – you <u>fool</u> – he <u>knows</u>. Of course he knows.'
3: Happiness	When Sheila accepts the engagement ring from Gerald	'Oh – it's <u>wonderful</u>! Look – Mummy – isn't it a <u>beauty</u>?'

5 a) bitter; b) impatient; c) sarcastic; d) frank

6 Sheila's tone of voice towards Gerald has changed from affection at the beginning of the play, to one of sarcasm in Act Two.

7

Example or quotation	Literary technique	Meaning/effect
1: The Inspector	Symbolism	He is the symbol of conscience, of our need to consider the welfare of others.
2: 'And one day, I hope, Eric, when you've a daughter of your own' (Act One, p. 4)	Dramatic irony	Mr Birling (and the audience) are unaware in Act One that Eva Smith was pregnant with Eric's child.
3: 'the girl's condition' (Act Three, p. 53)	Euphemism	The girl (Eva Smith) was pregnant.

8

Technique	Example	Effect
1: Repetition	'**We** don't live alone. **We** are members of one body. **We** are responsible for each other.'	Stresses key words. The pronoun 'we' emphasises our shared responsibility
2: Long and short sentences in succession	Long sentence ending: 'we think and say and do.' Three short sentences follow: 'We don't live alone' etc.	Long sentences show a rapid flow of ideas. Short sentence stresses a key idea. Different sentence lengths can change the tone and can, for example, add tension
3: Metaphor	'in fire and blood and anguish'	Represents 'conflict' or 'war'. Expresses strong feelings

Structure [p. 54]

1

Scene	Act
1: The Inspector questions Mrs Birling	Two
2: Mr Birling rings Colonel Roberts	Three
3: The Inspector arrives	One
4: The Inspector's final speech	Three
5: Gerald leaves the stage after he's been questioned	Two
4: We learn that Eric has stolen money	Three

2 a) Tension builds as Sheila realises that Gerald knew Daisy Renton/Eva Smith. The Act ends dramatically, ready for Gerald's revelations in Act Two.

b) Questions are raised about whether or not the Inspector really is a police inspector. There is a second telephone call to say an inspector is arriving.

c) The Inspector decides who will be questioned and when, so controlling what is revealed. He uses the photograph and diary to control the information about Eva Smith.

PART SIX: GRADE BOOSTER [pp. 56–63]

Writing skills [pp. 56–7]

2 Student A: Level – *Mid*

Why? The student supports what he/she says with evidence and quotations, makes relevant comments and analyses some parts of the text closely, but the writing could be more fluent.

Student B: Level – *Higher*

Why? The student analyses the effect of specific words, selects quotations carefully and embeds them fluently in sentences. The writing is persuasive and the points made are convincing.

3 *The word 'inspector', as Eric uses it, suggests the Birlings were thoroughly investigated.*

4, 5, 6

*J. B. Priestley **conveys** the depth of Eric's misery when he accuses Mr Birling of not being 'the kind of father a chap could go to when he's in trouble'. It not only **implies** that there is little trust between the two, and **reveals** a father to whom Eric cannot admit weakness, it also **suggests** Mr Birling is an unsympathetic man.*

Spelling, punctuation and grammar [pp. 58–9]

3 *At the end of Act Two, the **tension** builds **dramatically** as Mrs Birling, '**exchanges** a frightened glance with her husband', and they **realise** that Eric has been involved with Eva Smith. By the time the curtain falls, J. B. Priestley ensures that the **audience** knows that Eric is the likely father of Eva Smith's unborn child.*

4 *When Priestley gives the Inspector the name of 'Goole', we think of the word 'ghoul', which is another word for 'ghost' or '**phantom**'. Since the Inspector is a mysterious figure and as Gerald discovers in Act Three, '**wasn't a police officer**', the name 'Goole' may well have been Priestley's special choice.*

5 Student B

6 *Sheila **tries** to make her mother understand that she **is** building, 'a kind of wall' between the family 'and that girl', Eva Smith. The word 'wall' **is** an image Priestley **uses** to imply a barrier that Mrs Birling **is** constructing to protect herself from admitting the truth.*

Planning and structure [p 61]

3 *How does <u>J. B. Priestley</u> <u>depict</u> the <u>relationship</u> between <u>workers</u> and <u>employers</u> in the play?*

4, 5

c) *He depicts how Eva Smith as an employee was at the mercy of Birling and Company if she went on strike for higher wages.*

'Birling: … And this girl, Eva Smith, was one of them [ringleaders]. She'd had a lot to say – far too much – so she had to go.'

d) *He depicts how easily Milwards sacked Eva Smith regardless of her good record as an employee.*

'Inspector: There was nothing wrong with the way she [Eva Smith] was doing her work [at Milwards]. … All she knew was – that a customer complained about her – and so she had to go.'

e) *Priestley shows the double standards Mr Birling uses when Eric, who has a position at Birlings, steals from the company.*

'Birling: Gave the firm's receipt and then kept the money, eh? … You must give me the list of those accounts. I've got to cover this up as soon as I can.'

Sample answers [pp. 62–3]

1 Student A: Expert viewpoint 1; **Student B:** Expert viewpoint 2

3 Student A: Expert viewpoint 2; **Student B:** Expert viewpoint 1